AGILE ADOPTION FOR DIGITAL TRANSFORMATION IN THE IT SECTOR

A Thesis

Dr. RAJESH PRAMOD PATNURI

B.Tech., MBA, MS, PhD

Woven Words Publishers OPC Pvt. Ltd.

Registered Office:

Vill: Raipur, P.O: Raipur Paschimbar,

Dist: Purba Midnapore, Pin: 721401,

West Bengal, India.

Branch Office (Operations): Hyderabad

www.wovenwordspublishers.com

Email: publish@wovenwordspublishers.com

First published by Woven Words Publishers OPC Pvt. Ltd., 2023

Price: Rs. 599/-

IMPRINT: WOVEN WORDS ACADEMIC

ISBN 13: 9789391209001
ISBN 10: 93-91209-00-9
Book size: 6*9

ABSTRACT

Faster delivery of business value is a struggle for many IT businesses because of VUCA (volatile, uncertain, complex, and ambiguous) challenges. The traditional ways of managing and delivering services are no longer efficient at dealing with the VUCA challenges. Agile is a modern delivery methodology that may be used, however if an IT firm makes the decision to switch to Agile, they will face several transformation challenges. This research focused on the role of Agile leadership during the Agile transformation in IT organizations, identify the challenges they face, how Agile implementation can help overcome these challenges, identify techniques to sustain Agility and the importance of Agile frameworks for business agility and digital transformation. This research was limited to web-based surveys with experts in the field of Agile in IT organizations. There was some generic Agile questionnaire in the survey, according to the responses, the most practiced Agile framework is 'Scrum', the main reason for adopting Agile is 'regular feedback cycle increases value creation' and the main challenge faced during Agile transformation is 'lack of collaboration'. Rest of the survey questionnaire were recorded on Likert Scale and qualitative methodology was used to analyze the data and results. Reliability test was conducted to find the stability and consistency, the reliability result inferred as Excellent. Mean, standard deviation, variance is calculated as part of the statistical analysis. Pearson correlation and multiple regression analysis was conducted to test the hypothesis, this research confirms that, overcoming the Agile adoption challenges is important, Agile Leader and coaches are critical success factors, sustaining Agility is important, Agile methodologies (ex: Scrum, SAFe & other Agile frameworks) are key success factors and Agile adoption is key for enterprise business agility & digital transformation.

Key Words: Agile, Agile Leadership, Agile Project Management, Agile Coaching, Agile HR, Agile Marketing, Agile Transformation, Digital Transformation, Scrum, DevOps

TABLE OF CONTENTS

Page

LIST OF TABLES

LIST OF FIGURES

Figure Page

CHAPTER 1

1. INTRODUCTION

First of all, we will understand the meaning of Agile.

Agile: What does it mean? below are the meanings according to OxfordLearnersDictionaries.com. (n.d.).

1. easy to move and move quickly
2. capable of thinking quickly and smartly
3. used to describe a way to manage projects in which work is broken up into short tasks and there are regular breaks to look at the work and make changes
4. used to describe a way of working in which the time, place, and roles of people can all change depending on what needs to be done and the focus is on the goals to be reached instead of the exact methods used (OxfordLearnersDictionaries.com, n.d.)

Agile is a term for software development that has made it into the business world. The steps of the scientific method have a lot in common with Agile approaches. There is some overlap in what they are meant to do, but there is also a big difference. Even though both science and software development try to find the truth—science to find a better, relative truth and software development to express the reality of the initial project specifications—Agile techniques are mostly concerned with making the development process as productive as possible (Damlapinar, 2022).

1.1. Traditional and Agile Models

1.1.1. Waterfall Model

The waterfall model is the oldest and most basic traditional software development methodology. In this approach, the entire software development process is divided into linear sequential phases. In each phase, a deliverable must be completed before moving on to the next phase. The first phase is known as the requirements gathering phase wherein analysts and customers work together to identify what the product should do. This is followed by the design phase wherein engineers create a blueprint of how the product will work. In the next phase, known as the implementation/development or coding phase, developers write code according to the specifications laid out in the design phase. Once the code is complete, it moves on to the testing phase where testers check for bugs and errors. After all errors have been fixed, the product is ready for launch in the market during deployment phase, later product will be maintained until it is needed for business. (Petersen, Wohlin & Baca, 2009).

Figure 1. 1 Waterfall Model

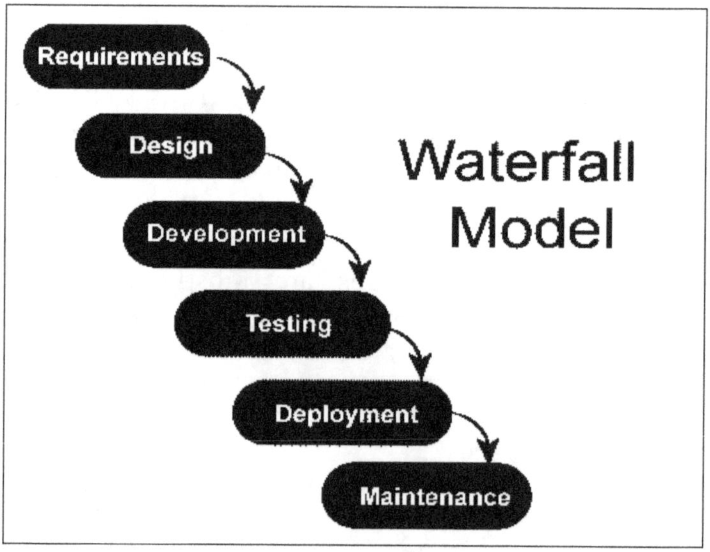

Source: www.medium.com

The widespread use of the waterfall method may be due, in part, to pure inertia. The majority of system developers are familiar with it because it has been used on so many projects over the last few decades. The waterfall approach's dominance is due in part to the structure's logic. The life cycle of a project flows logically from feasibility through requirements analysis, a design phase, an implement-and-test phase (sometimes incorporating programming), through acceptance, and after delivery into the maintenance phase. This sequential paradigm is straightforward, and the order of the phases is clear to understand (Light, 2009).

The biggest benefit of the waterfall model is that it is easy to understand and use. This model is best suited for small and non-complex projects where requirements are well understood. Additionally, this model also provides detailed documentation of the entire process which can be later used for reference or training purposes. Finally, since all phases are completed one after the other, there is no need to go back and make changes in earlier phases, which saves time and effort. Waterfall model has a number of disadvantages. Firstly, it does not allow for much flexibility and is not suitable for projects where requirements are subject to change. Secondly, since all phases must be completed before moving on to the next level. The waterfall model is very rigid and does not allow for much flexibility or revision (Light, 2009).

1.1.2. V-model

The V-model is a more Agile (compared to waterfall model) and efficient way to develop software. It allows for more collaboration and feedback, which leads to better quality products. The V-model also enables teams to quickly respond to changes in customer needs. It is based on verification and validation of each phase in the software development process that helps identify issues earlier, reducing risk and increasing quality assurance. By following this model, teams can create a comprehensive plan that guides them through every step of the process, helping to ensure smooth operation of the software product at all stages. Through the use of rapid feedback cycles, the V-model encourages quick iteration and adaptation while maintaining control over project progress and outcomes. This makes it an ideal choice for companies seeking to speed up their software delivery cycle without sacrificing quality or reliability. Ultimately, the V-model's structured approach offers organizations a reliable way to develop high quality software products faster than ever before (Johansson & Bucanac, 1999).

The V-model offers organizations the flexibility to customize each phase of the software development process according to their specific needs and requirements. This is accomplished by providing teams with a series of checkpoints they must meet in order to move on to the next step in the process. Each stage has a set of objectives that must be met, enabling teams to quickly adapt when customer or market needs change. These checkpoints also help ensure quality assurance is maintained throughout the development cycle and provide an easy way for teams to measure progress against goals. Additionally, the V-model encourages collaboration between all parts of the organization, from product owners and developers, to testers and business users. By maintaining close contact between stakeholders, problems can be identified early within projects which helps to avoid costly delays and rework (Johansson & Bucanac, 1999).

Figure 1. 2 V-Model

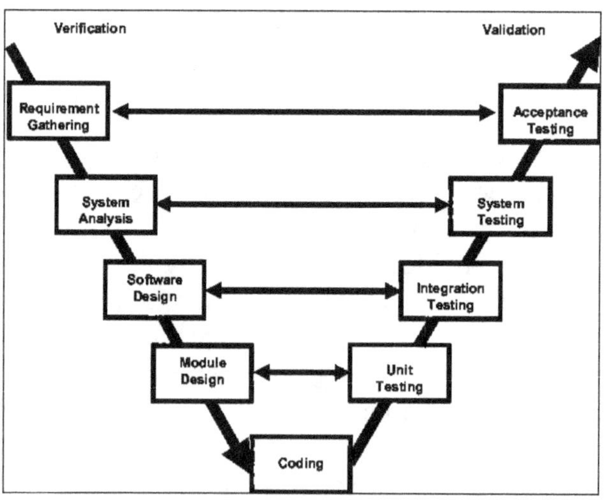

Source: www.medium.com

The V-model has proven to be an effective way for organizations to develop high quality software products. By following this process, teams can move quickly through the development stages while maintaining control over progress and outcomes. Additionally, its structured approach encourages collaboration across all parts of the organization, enabling teams to stay informed on project progress and pivot when needed. Ultimately, the V-model enables organizations to create better software faster, reducing risks and increasing efficiency in the development cycle. The benefits of using a V-model in software development are numerous. Not only is it easier to structure projects around customer or market needs but teams also have access to improved feedback cycles that allow them to identify and address problems quickly. Additionally, it ensures that each phase of the process is carefully monitored and validated so that quality assurance is maintained throughout. Ultimately, the V-model provides organizations with a reliable way to create better software faster without sacrificing quality or reliability. This makes it an ideal choice for any organization looking to speed up its development cycle while still producing high quality products. With its flexibility and quick iteration capabilities, the V-model has revolutionized software development processes in many industries today. By taking advantage of this streamlined approach, organizations can maximize productivity and minimize risk when deploying new projects (Yadav, 2012).

1.1.3. Spiral Model

The spiral model is an evolution of the waterfall model. In this approach, the software development process is divided into four distinct phases: Planning, Risk Analysis, Engineering and Evaluation. Each phase builds upon the previous one and allows for revision and feedback at each stage (Boehm, 1995).

Figure 1. 3 Spiral Model

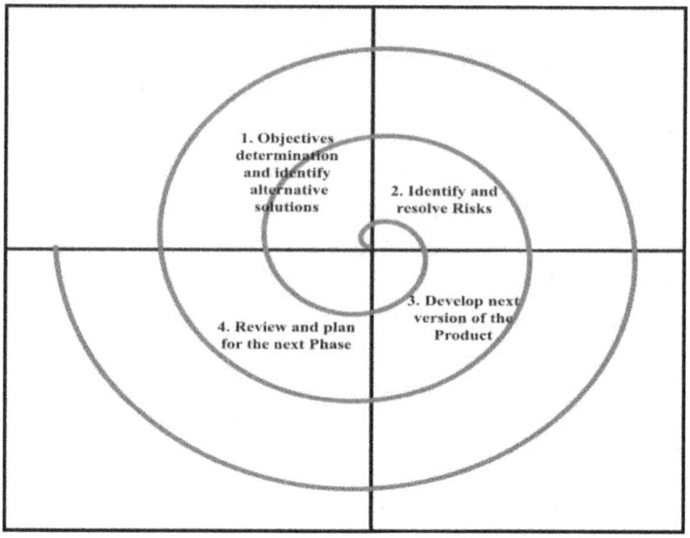

Source: https://www.geeksforgeeks.org/

The spiral model is the perfect solution for managing software development projects. This model allows for planning, risk analysis, engineering and evaluation throughout each phase of the project cycle in order to ensure successful completion within budget and timeline constraints. With this approach, you can rest assured that your project will be completed efficiently without any surprises along the way (Boehm, 1995).

1.1.4. Agile

The Agile is a new approach that has gained popularity in recent years. In this approach, the software development process is divided into short cycles, or sprints. Each sprint is typically two weeks long and focuses on a specific deliverable. The Agile methodology is very flexible and allows for constant revision and feedback. IT organizations are always under pressure to deliver business value faster and more efficiently. Agile provides a framework for achieving these goals, but many IT organizations struggle with Agile implementation. Agile can help IT organizations overcome the challenges of business and digital transformation and achieve their desired outcomes. An Agile business goes beyond simply aligning to the Agile methodology. Agility is the bedrock of digital transformation (Perkin & Abraham, 2021).

In contrast to the conventional methods (waterfall, v-model & spiral model), Agile is a set of beliefs and concepts that aims to provide software more incrementally and iteratively. Working in an Agile manner have lot of advantages, including enhanced team communication, quicker software delivery, and increased customer satisfaction. Agile enables shorter development cycles and more adaptability to changes. However, adopting Agile is not always simple, and businesses must be mindful of any potential dangers. IT firms are under pressure to shift digitally or else risk becoming obsolete. Many people are using Agile to accelerate their transformational endeavors. Using Agile for digital transformation has several advantages. First, it makes firms more Agile and adaptable to change. Second, it promotes cross-functional cooperation and teamwork. Third, it gives businesses the ability to test ideas rapidly and learn from them, which is crucial for a successful digital transition (Campanelli & Parreiras, 2015).

1.2. Agile Adoption

Agile adoption can bring a number of benefits to organizations, including improved communication and collaboration, faster time to market and more satisfied customers. Additionally, Agile methods can help reduce costs and improve quality. When adopting Agile methods, it is important to remember that there is no one-size-fits-all solution. The approach that works best for an organization will depend on its specific needs and culture (Moreira, 2013).

However, there are some general guidelines that can help ensure a successful transition to Agile.

- Establish a clear vision and objectives for the transition.
- Create a dedicated team responsible for overseeing the transition.

- ➢ Train all employees in the basics of Agile methods.
- ➢ Implement Agile methods incrementally, starting with small projects.
- ➢ Monitor progress closely and make adjustments as needed.

By following these tips, organizations can increase the likelihood of a successful Agile adoption. Business executives are not usually cognizant of how IT assists the running of a business, since they often consider the technology leader as a subservient role. As a result, the demands on IT frequently exceed the IT budget, the IT department frequently lacks organization, and financial, technical, and human resources are not always in line with the organization's primary objectives. DevSecOps in particular, an Agile practice, aids in bringing about this alignment (Mohammad, 2017).

1.3. Benefits of Agile Adoption

According to Jack (2018), there are five types of organization cultures exist - **Teal**, **Green**, **Orange**, **Amber** and **Red.**

Red organizations are those that are motivated by power and control. They tend to be highly hierarchical in structure and have strong rules about how things get done.

Amber organizations are focused on providing services and products to their customers. They believe that their customers should be satisfied with what they offer and will keep coming back for more.

Orange organizations are focused on making money. They believe that if they make a profit, they can use that money to help others.

Green organizations are focused on the environment and social responsibility. They believe that it is important to do what is best for the planet and the people who live on it.

Figure 1. 4 Organizational Altitudes

Organizational Altitudes (or Value Cultures)

Evolutionary / Purpose-driven (Teal)	***Focus on inner integrity, sees systemically*** Dis-identifies with own ego, purpose-driven, authenticity Inner Rightness as Compass, Wisdom beyond Rationality
Pluralistic / Relationship-driven (Green)	***Fairness, community, equality of all perspectives*** Focus on justice for all, consensus, relationship over outcomes *Empowerment, Values-driven culture, Multi-Stakeholder perspective*
Achievement / Results-driven (Orange)	***Pragmatic, success-oriented, complex logic*** Questions authority, get ahead, values freedom & achievement *Innovation, Accountability, Meritocracy*
Conformist / Role-driven (Amber)	***Awareness of social roles, following authority*** Absolute Truth (black & white), can see other's expectations, dogmatic *Long-term perspective, Consistent Process, Size & Stability (Hierarchy)*
Implusive (Red)	***Power & dominance, heroism, avoidance of shame*** Separate ego, dominance vs submission, chiefdoms, illegal orgs

Source: Frederic Laloux – Reinventing Organizations, plus Wilber, Graves, Beck, and Cook-Greuter

Finally, **Teal** organizations are those that have a very strong focus on the people who work there. They believe that if the employees are happy, the company will be successful.

Each type of organization has its own unique advantages and disadvantages, so it is important to consider your organizational needs when deciding which type is right for you. No matter which type of organization you choose, having a clear set of goals, objectives, values, and strategies can help ensure success. Additionally, effective communication within the workplace is essential in order to ensure employees understand expectations while fostering collaboration between team members. Having diverse teams with different insights and perspectives can help bring new ideas to the table, leading to more innovative solutions. Finally, investing in employee development will ensure that your organization has an engaged and productive workforce. With these considerations in mind, you can be sure that you are choosing the right type of organization for your business's needs. Agile adoption can help organizations to transform towards **Teal**, which makes it evolutionally and purpose driven organization (Jack, 2018).

There are four main areas where Agile can help IT organizations improve their business and digital transformation (Guinan, Parise, & Langowitz, 2019):

1. **Processes:** Many IT organizations have legacy processes that are not well suited for Agile. Agile can help streamline these processes and make them more effective.
2. **Culture:** IT culture is often resistant to change. Agile can help create a more open and collaborative culture that is more conducive to business organizations.
3. **Governance:** IT governance structures are often too rigid to accommodate Agile. Agile can help create more flexible governance structures that can support business and digital transformation.
4. **Technology:** IT organizations often have legacy technology systems that may not be well suited for them. Agile can help modernize these systems and help them in business and digital transformation.

Traditional project management methodologies like water fall, spiral model give false sense of time predictability where Agile methodologies provides a good predictability based on experience which is called empiricism.

The other benefit of Agile is helping to create Holacratic organizational culture. There are various types of corporate cultures:

The most typical organizational culture is **hierarchical**; it has existed for thousands of years and is often referred to as a "line organization." The power is transferred from the board of directors to the rest of the company through a top-to-bottom chain of command.

Flatarchy: A flatter organizational structure removes tiers inside the business and facilitates communication and teamwork.

Holacracy: The Holacratic organizational structure is made up of a set of rules that, by giving all employees—rather than just the management—the ability to innovate, make changes, and speak up, can promote the practice of self-organization and self-management. Consequently, an organization might implement a

Holacratic culture to enable the innovation, transformation and good quality (Lopez Martín de Blas, n.d.).

1.4. Role of Agile Leadership

Leadership is critical in any organization, but it is especially important when implementing Agile methods. Leaders need to provide guidance and direction during the transition, and they need to be champions of the new approach. Additionally, leaders need to be aware of the potential challenges that can occur during an Agile implementation. They need to be prepared to address these challenges if they arise. Agile can help IT organizations overcome the challenges of business and digital transformation and deliver business value faster and more efficiently. If companies are looking to improve the organization's Agile implementation, they should first secure support from all interested parties. Second, throughout the transition period, they need to be ready for some confusion and disturbance. Third, they must make sure they have the resources and tools necessary to support Agile in place. Agile offers a lot of advantages for transformation in IT companies that can help organizations increase their bottom line. Agile technique, for instance, reduces the time it takes for new goods and services to reach the market. Agile also enables businesses to better manage change and get rid of waste, which can assist lower development costs. Finally, Agile fosters better teamwork and communication, which can result in more fruitful project outputs. The need of the hour is business agility, not just delivery process and engineering agility or even IT agility (Narayan, 2015).

1.5. Agile Adoption Challenges

While there are a number of benefits that can be realized by organizations when they adopt Agile methods, there are also some challenges that need to be considered. Some of these challenges include employee resistance to change, lack of understanding of Agile methods, implementation failures due to inadequate planning, and difficulty measuring success. Some tips for overcoming these challenges include:

1. *Communicating the vision and objectives for the transition to all employees:* It is important that employees are aware of the reasons for the change to Agile methods and what is expected of them during the transition. Leaders should take the time to communicate this information to all employees, as well as provide training on the basics of Agile methods. Agile transition requires sufficient time and effort and is frequently hampered by a number of obstacles, largely because it is people-centric (Javdani Gandomani, & Ziaei Nafchi, 2016).

2. *Creating a dedicated team responsible for overseeing the transition:* A dedicated team can help to ensure that the transition to Agile methods goes smoothly. This team should be responsible for planning and implementing the transition, as well as monitoring progress and making adjustments as needed (Poth, Kottke, & Riel, 2020).

3. *Implementing Agile methods incrementally, starting with small projects:* It is often easier to transition to Agile methods if they are implemented incrementally, starting with small projects. This allows employees to get used to the new methods and processes gradually. Additionally, it helps to ensure that any issues that arise can be quickly identified and addressed (Kaur & Jajoo, 2015).

4. *Measuring success using a variety of metrics:* A variety of metrics can be used to assess the success of an Agile adoption. Some of these metrics include customer satisfaction, delivery time, quality, and cost. Leaders should choose the metrics that are most important for their organization and track progress over time (Kandengwa & Khoza, 2021).

There is no one-size-fits-all Agile technique; instead, it must be customized to fit into already-existing processes (Mahanti, 2006).

1.6. Research Context

It is now globally evident that Business and Technology are inextricably linked, with businesses requiring more agility to compete and win in an ever-changing marketplace. Increasingly, senior business leaders are turning to IT organizations to help them drive business transformation. Agile provides a framework for achieving these goals, but many IT organizations struggle with its implementation. Companies should overcome the challenges of Agile implementation and achieve their desired outcomes.

1.7. Research Problem

For businesses all around the world, digital transformation (DT) is becoming increasingly important. Traditional and manual business operations are predicted to fail and stagnate, eventually going out of business, whereas businesses making the switch to the digital economy are predicted to be competitive and robust to advancements in technology (Elacio, Balazon, & Lacatan, 2020).

While many IT organizations are under pressure to deliver business value faster and more efficiently, they often struggle with the implementation of Agile due to legacy processes, inflexible governance structures, and outdated technology systems. This study will analyze the effectiveness of Agile in business and digital transformation of IT firms in order to address that research challenge. This research will explore how Agile can help IT organizations overcome these challenges and improve their business and digital transformation. IT organizations can greatly enhance their business and digital transformation processes by implementing Agile. It enables companies to be more flexible and sensitive to change, which is crucial in today's constantly shifting environment. Agile can also help firms deliver high-quality goods and services while saving time and money.

1.8. The Significance of the Research

This research is important because it will provide insights into how Agile can help IT organizations improve their business and digital transformation. This research is also significant because it will contribute to our understanding of how Agile can facilitate organizational change.

1.9. Scope of Study

This research will focus on role of Agile adoption and role of Agile leadership in business and digital transformation in the context of IT organizations. This research will not explore Agile implementations in other types of organizations which are not in IT sector. Additionally, this research will be limited to surveys with experts in the field of Agile. This research will employ a qualitative methodology, utilizing interviews with experts in the field of business and digital transformation. These experts will be asked about their experiences helping IT organizations improve their Agile implementations. The data collected will be analyzed to identify common themes and patterns. It is expected that this research will provide insights into how business and digital transformation can help IT organizations improve their Agile implementations. Specifically, this research will identify the challenges that IT organizations face and how Agile implementation can help overcome these challenges in business and digital transformation. Additionally, this research will explore the benefits that IT organizations can realize by investing in business and digital transformation.

1.10. Research Objectives

The goal of this research is to understand how Agile can help IT organizations improve the business and digital transformation. The goal of this research is to investigate how Agile methodologies are being used in companies to provide business and digital transformation and to pinpoint any weaknesses or difficulties in the current methods. A review of the current literature as well as structured questionnaires and surveys with subject-matter experts will be used to conduct the research. The research's conclusions will be utilized to create suggestions for enhancing the delivery of business and digital transformation in firms that adopt Agile methodologies. Specifically, this research will:

1) Identify the challenges that IT organizations face during Agile transformation.
2) Role of Agile Leadership & Agile Coach in Agile transformation.
3) Identify the techniques to sustain as Agile enterprise.
4) Role of Agile methodologies in business & digital transformation of IT companies.
5) Agile adoption in IT organizations foster business agility and overcome the digital transformation challenges.

These objectives will be used to find the literature and primary data.

1.11. Research Questions

Below are the high-level research questions of the study.

1) What are the challenges that IT organizations face while Agile transformation?
2) What is the role of Agile Leadership & Agile Coach in Agile Transformation?
3) What are the techniques in order to sustain as an Agile enterprise?
4) Whether Agile methodologies help and/or appropriate in business & digital transformation of IT companies?
5) Whether Agile adoption help IT organizations to achieve business agility overcome the business and digital transformation challenges?

These questions served to break down into survey questionnaire to collect the secondary data which used to test the hypothesis.

1.12. Research Hypothesis

Below are the null hypotheses of the study.

1) Overcoming Agile adoption challenges is not important to implement Agile and transform as an Agile Enterprise
2) Agile Leadership and Agile Coaching are not critical success factors in adopting Agile & transformation in IT Companies
3) Sustaining as Agile enterprise is not important in digital era
4) Agile methodologies are not key success factors for business & digital transformation
5) Agile adoption is not key to achieve enterprise business agility and overcome digital transformation challenges

Figure 1. 5 Conceptual Framework

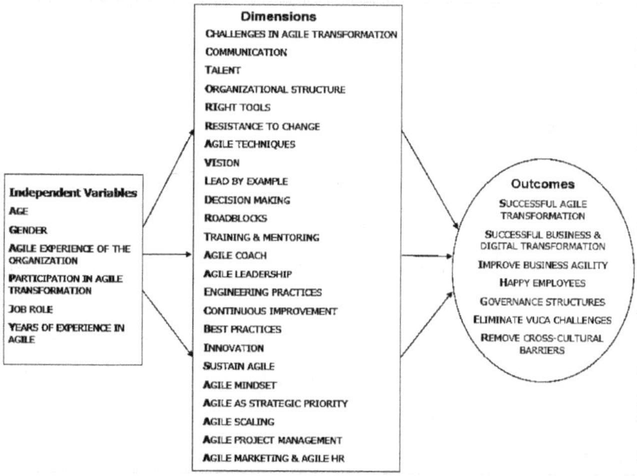

Source: Patnuri, 2023

As shown in the above figure, by using independent variables and dimensions (which include dependent variables), null hypotheses will be tested further in this research.

1.13. Outline of Chapters

The following outline summarizes the research dissertation chapters.

1. Introduction – Consists of introduction to the study, purpose of research, objectives and hypothesis
2. Theoritical Framework – Provides theoritical concepts related to research topic and methodologies.
3. Review of Literature – Discusses about the literature aligned to the research objectives
4. Research Methodology – Discusses about the approach to the research methodology, data colection and analysis tools
5. Data Analysis & Interpretation – Discusses about the data analysis and interpretation of results
6. Findings and Recommendations – Summary of research findings and recommendations in researcher point of view
7. Discussion and Implications – Summary of research implications
8. Conclusion – Research conclusion
9. Bibliography – Summary of references.

Above chapters will be described in detail in this dissertation.

CHAPTER 2

2. THEORETICAL FRAMEWORK

2.1. Agile Adoption

Agile is a mindset with set of software development methodologies and frameworks that has revolutionized the way businesses approach software development. Agile was first introduced in the early 2000s, and has since become one of the most popular development methodologies in use today. Agile is based on a set of principles that emphasize collaboration, customer feedback, and iterative development. These principles are meant to promote a more efficient and effective software development process. The Agile methodologies has been incredibly successful in helping businesses create better software faster. In fact, many of the world's most successful companies use Agile methods to develop their products (Lang, 2017).

2.1.1. Why to adopt Agile?

Professor Manuel Lopez Martin de Blas (n.d.) claims that 31% of all IT projects are abandoned before they are finished, 53% of those that are finished cost an average of 189% more than what was originally budgeted, and 55% of those that are finished provided an average of 42% of the features that were initially proposed (Lopez Martin de Blas, n.d.).

According to Perminova, Gustafsson, & Wikström (2008), the following are some common causes of risk for IT projects:

1) **Integration:** A lack of post-project appraisal, insufficient planning, inappropriate resource allocation, and ineffective integration management

2) **Scope:** Poor or incomplete scope or work package specifications
3) **Time:** Problems with critical path determination, assessment of time or resource availability, and insufficient time allocation
4) **Cost:** Overestimated productivity, undercharged costs, unanticipated changes, or contingencies
5) **Quality:** Inadequate design, materials, and workmanship; insufficient quality assurance processes; poor attitudes toward quality; and
6) **Human Resources:** A lack of leadership, unclear project organization and responsibilities, and poor conflict resolution
7) **Communication:** Inattention to detail in preparation or communication
8) **Risk:** Neglecting risk considerations, interpreting risks poorly, and managing insurance poorly
9) **Procurement:** Unenforceable clauses or provisions in contracts that lead to conflict
10) **Stakeholders:** Poor sponsor participation as a result of lack of communication with important stakeholders

Adopting Agile framework/s (with the support of Agile Leaders and under coaching of Agile coach) the problems described above can be minimized. Agile frameworks such as Scrum, SAFe, and LeSS, among others, introduce a culture of working that will assist minimize the aforementioned problems.

Agile software development is a collection of iterative and incremental software development approaches, in which requirements and solutions are developed in collaboration among self-organizing cross-functional teams. Agile software development is also sometimes referred to as lean software development. Agile methods and approaches encourage sustainable development, customer satisfaction through the early and continual delivery of valuable software, and close, day-to-day collaboration between business people and software engineers. Early attempts at using Agile approaches in software development were often called light methodology, which was an attempt to distance these new methods from the more traditional heavyweight waterfall methods that were common at the time. The term Agile has since become widely accepted in the software development community.

Agile methods or approaches can be used in various different ways, from very loosely defined frameworks like Scrum to more prescriptive ones like Extreme Programming (XP). There is no one size fits all approach to Agile software development, and teams should choose the method or approach that best suits their needs. Agile is not a silver bullet for all software development projects, and it is not always the best approach. However, it can be very effective for projects that are characterized by uncertainty or rapidly changing requirements (Fernandez & Fernandez, 2008).

According to Cuofano (2022), for the business to succeed, the departments of HR, Finance, Operations, Marketing, and Legal must coordinate their efforts. The phrase "**survive, compete, and thrive**" might be used to describe the culture of adoptability in this situation. In the end, this mentality aids an organization in transitioning from its present condition to a desirable, Agile state.

2.1.2. Origins of Agile

The traditional waterfall software development paradigm has a number of drawbacks, including rigid phase sequencing, a heavy reliance on documents, advance planning of the process, and little flexibility for needs changes (Hajjdiab & Taleb, 2011).

In the early 1990s, a group of software developers came together with the goal of improving the efficiency of the software development process. They took inspiration from various sources, including Lean Manufacturing, Toyota Production System, and Agile Modeling. They developed a set of principles that they called the Agile Manifesto. The Manifesto has four main values: ***Individuals and interactions over processes and tools***; ***Working software over comprehensive documentation***; ***Customer collaboration over contract negotiation***; and ***Responding to change over following a plan***. These values have helped to shape the Agile Methodology, which is now used by many software developments teams around the world (Abbas, Gravell & Wills, 2008).

Figure 2. 1 Agile Manifesto

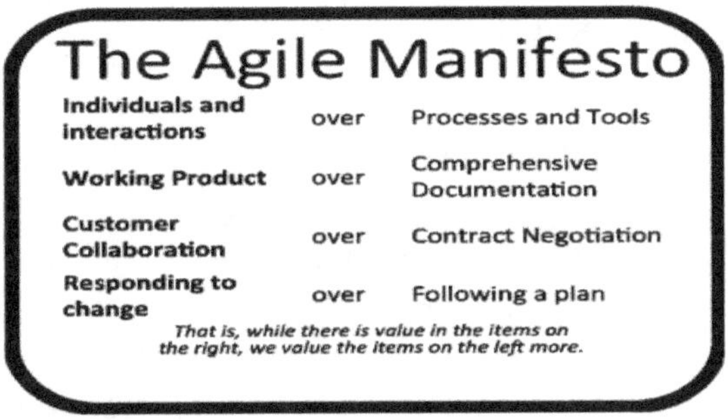

The four values of Agile manifesto are shown in the above figure.

There are 12 Principles behind Agile Manifesto. Those 12 principles are shown in the below figure (Principles Behind the Agile Manifesto, n.d.).

Figure 2. 2 Twelve Agile Principles

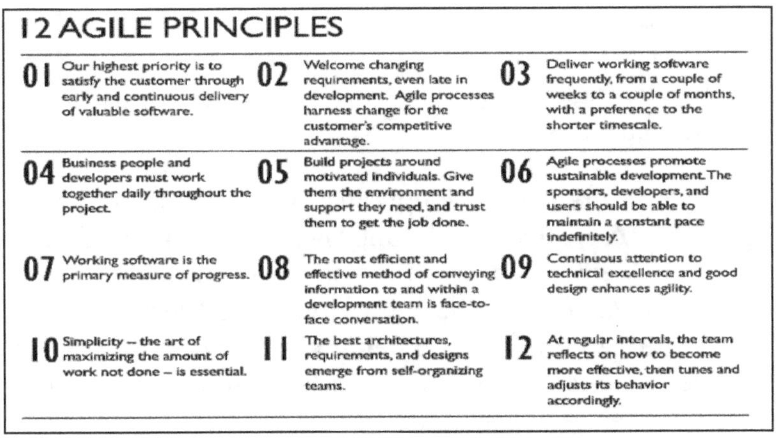

Source: https://nicocasel.net/

In recent years, the Agile Methodology has been increasingly adopted by organizations outside of the software development industry, as its emphasis on flexibility and adaptation has proven to be valuable in a variety of fields. While it has evolved over the years, the core principles of Agile remain the same: focus on customer needs, embrace change, and deliver working software quickly. Thanks to its focus on speed and flexibility, Agile has become the go-to methodology for developing software in today's rapidly changing world (Conforto, Edivandro C., et al, 2014).

2.1.3. Main Elements of Agile

Agile is a process that helps organizations manage and deliver projects in a more flexible and effective way. It is based on the principle of continuous improvement and focuses on delivering value to the customer through early and frequent delivery of working software. The Agile process is typically carried out using a set of specific practices and tools, which vary depending on the particular approach being used. However, some common Agile practices include:

1) Iterative development
2) Time boxing
3) Self-organizing teams
4) Continuous integration
5) Test-driven development
6) Agile modeling
7) User stories

Organizations that adopt an Agile approach to project management typically see improved communication and collaboration between team members, as well as increased customer satisfaction and faster delivery of working software products. Agile approaches are being adopted by more and more software development companies in order to boost software quality and speed (Özkan & Mishra, 2019).

2.1.4. Steps in Agile Transformation

According to Spayd and Madore (2020), Agile transformation is a 5-step process. Agile Transformation Leader or Agile Coach should demonstrate these competencies for a successful enterprise Agile transformation. Below is the detailed explanation of this 5-step process and the associated sub processes.

Step#1: GUIDING THE CHANGE TRANSFORMATION PROCESS

1.1. Understands Organizational Structures

Has a methodical approach to interacting with organizational processes. Establishes ties with the client by identifying them. Clarifies the business case and the reasons for the change with the client. Build a coalition in support of the business case by working with all significant stakeholders. Defines the nature and extent of the alterations.

1.2. Evaluates organizational structures

Shows the capacity to evaluate and make apparent the system's current condition. Assessment examines the system from a variety of angles. Explains the difference between the present and the future condition. Provides enough detail to direct further actions.

1.3. Co-creates the transformation strategy

Shows aptitude for using a methodical, group-based approach to change design that strikes a balance between general trends and client-specific objectives. The method bridges the gaps between the present and the desired future states and is co-created with the client. It should cover issues with corporate agility and human systems, as well as the crucial interaction between culture and leadership.

1.4. Aids businesses in bringing about and maintaining change

Demonstrates the capacity to lead the organization in putting the desired change into practice, adjusting to it, and maintaining it. implements the change approach. examines and modifies change initiatives in light of facts. Determines when to put specific components of the change process into sustainment mode in order to get ready for the coach to move his or her attention to other change initiatives.

Step#2: IMPROVE ORGANIZATIONAL LEADERSHIP

2.1 Encourages leadership growth at all levels

Demonstrates the capacity to encourage the growth of leadership across the organization, not only at the "management" level. Believes that rather than being a particular job, leadership is a role within functional institutions. They demonstrate appreciation for leadership displays outside the management ranks through their conduct. Works well with individuals at all organizational levels to develop their leadership.

2.2 Partners and guides to construct purposefully developed leadership programs

Ability to plan and implement leadership development initiatives in support of business results has been proven. able to explain the role that leadership plays in organizational transformation generally as well as the commercial case for vertical development. Be able to collaborate with internal stakeholder groups (HR, Learning & Development) as necessary to build or have effective vertical leadership development programs developed. is qualified to provide leadership coaching themselves or to support the employment of qualified, experienced professional coaches to do so.

Step#3: COACHING RANGE

3.1 Coaches Teams as Human Systems

Possesses adequate system knowledge and adopts a viewpoint that makes it clear when to coach individuals and when to train a human system. Shows awareness of the client as they are at any given time and purposefully switches to coaching from their perspective, whether they are an individual or a system. For the benefit of the operation and growth of the system, directly and successfully addresses the emergent features of systems.

3.2 Serves as a professional coach for individuals

Exhibits the capacity to collaborate in a stimulating and imaginative approach that motivates the client to realize their full potential both personally and professionally. Able to coach the complete spectrum of human emotions while maintaining their integrity and honesty. Decides consciously when to serve as a professional coach versus another stance.

3.3 Facilitates groupings outside of organizations

Demonstrates the capacity to collaborate effectively across organizational boundaries and with groups of various sizes. Maintains objectivity when acting in this capacity as a facilitator and has the ability to create cooperative group procedures that lead to clarity and alignment. Enables cross-border facilitation while taking organizational boundaries into account and is able to manage the complexity of many points of view.

3.4 Shows evidence of Agile coaching outside of organizational boundaries

Shows proficiency in Agile coaching at the senior leadership level and across several disciplines (technical, business, etc.) To ensure that the necessary assistance is given for the organizational change, one must be able to collaborate with other coaches and recognize their own capabilities across organizational levels and domains.

Step#4: EVOLVE YOURSELF AS A LEADER

4.1 Awareness of one's own abilities, limitations, and worldview

Demonstrates self-awareness by accurately assessing one's own strengths, faults, and belief systems as well as their effects on other people. The first step in improving oneself both personally and as a leader is increasing self-awareness. One can get more comfortable with their style of being when dealing with others through deliberate feedback systems and the capacity for introspection. One might see themselves as individuals who are not defined by others when they are self-aware.

4.2 Views, cultivates, and governs oneself as a transformative agent

Demonstrates an understanding that an Enterprise Coach can only advance a company's development to the extent of their own personal growth. They understand that they must go through metamorphosis themselves in order to help someone else. They are better equipped to assist others and consider others' viewpoints as a result. They are able to view individuals from more angles and view transformational methods from more views as well.

Exhibits the capacity to "stand in" one's own leadership while doing the duties of an enterprise coach. Their leadership is unambiguous, well-spoken, and consistent with their own ideals. They promote autonomy, serve as an example of it, and give others the option.

Step#5: GUIDING THE ENTERPRISE AGILITY

5.1 Works with sophisticated adaptive systems

Complexity theory, systems intelligence, systems thinking, and systems awareness are skills that are demonstrated. Adopt these concepts as part of their organizational agility strategy.

5.2 Helps with the creation of organizational structures

Helps to develop and co-create more flexible organizational structures to increase organizational agility. Includes feedback loops in organizational design to keep changing organizational structures as necessary during the change journey.

5.3 Directs the direction of methods, processes, and behaviors involved in product creation

Encourages habits and practices for collaborative product creation to promote organizational agility. Includes strategies that take into account every stakeholder and every voice inside the organizational system involved in the creation of products and services, including the customer.

5.4 Measures business results

Has the capacity to "measure what matters" and to explain how the results of the measurement impact agility. Can set up important qualitative and quantitative metrics for things like quality, flow and delivery, and prioritizing. Uses analytics to help, not as the end in mind. Detects and corrects undesired effects of certain metrics and measures while maintaining the broader business goals as the compass.

2.1.5. Main benefits of Agile

Some of the specific benefits that can be realized by organizations when they adopt Agile methods include (Niemi-Grundström, 2014):

1) **Improved communication and collaboration:** Agile methods promote communication and collaboration between all members of a project team. This can lead to better results as team

members are able to share ideas and information more effectively. Additionally, this improved communication can help to build trust among team members.

2) **Increased customer satisfaction:** One of the goals of Agile methods is to deliver working software to customers as quickly as possible. This can lead to increased customer satisfaction as they are able to receive the benefits of new features and functionality sooner.

3) **Faster time to market:** Agile methods also promote a faster time to market for new products and services. This is due to the fact that Agile methods focus on delivering working software incrementally. As a result, new products and services can be brought to market faster.

4) **Reduced costs:** Agile methods can help to reduce costs by reducing the amount of time and resources required for projects. Additionally, Agile methods can help reduce waste and improve efficiency.

5) **Improved quality:** Agile methods place an emphasis on quality throughout the software development process. This can lead to improved quality of the final product or service. Additionally, Agile methods can help to identify and fix defects sooner, which can further improve quality.

Overall, there are a number of benefits that can be realized by organizations when they adopt Agile methods. These benefits can lead to improved communication and collaboration, increased customer satisfaction, faster time to market, reduced costs, and improved quality.

2.1.6. Pros and Cons of Agile

Below table shows the pros and cons of Agile.

Table 2. 1 Agile Pros & Cons

Agile Pros	Agile Cons
Ability to handle shifting priorities	Resistance to embracing change
An improved project transparency	Teams could engage in inconsistent methods
Better alignment between IT and business	Requires assistance from management and leadership
Speed of delivery time to market	Agile values and organization culture may conflict
Ease of collaboration	Lack of documentation
Increased performance and productivity	Less predictability
Rapid delivery	Lack of overall cohesion

Source: Veritis (2022)

2.1.7. Constraints of Agile

According to Turk, France & Rumpe (2014), Agile has four major limitations as below:

- It is a methodology that prioritizes people and interactions over procedures and tools,
- Instead of extensive documentation, Agile emphasizes working software, flexible planning, evolutionary development, and early delivery.
- Agile emphasizes close cooperation between the development team and the client during the contract negotiation process.
- Agile prioritizes adapting to change over sticking to a plan. Agile is iterative, which means that it continuously improves.

With the first limitation being the most significant, these restrictions are designed to be applied in order of priority.

2.2. Agile Mindset

Agile mindset is, adopting set of tools, processes, practices, principles and values. This makes to move towards learning teams and learning organizations (Anonymous, n.d.).

Agile enables organizations to be more responsive to change, while still maintaining high quality standards. For a successful implementation of Agile, first, it is important to have a clear understanding of the principles behind Agile development. Second, you will need to select the right Agile framework for your organization. And finally, you will need to put in place the necessary tools and processes to support an Agile workflow (McDonald, 2015).

- By delivering working software incrementally, Agile teams can get feedback from customers early and often. This helps ensure that the final product meets customer needs and expectations.
- Agile projects are typically managed using visual tools like burn-down charts, which give everyone on the team a clear understanding of the project's progress. This transparency helps avoid surprises and keeps everyone aligned with the project's goals.
- By breaking projects down into smaller increments, Agile teams can identify and address risks early on. This helps avoid costly delays and rework later in the project.
- Agile methodology encourages close collaboration between all members of the project team. This improved communication leads to better-quality software and happier team members.

2.2.1. Attitude Inherited from Agility

The Agile approach is often contrasted with the more traditional waterfall approach to software development. The waterfall approach is characterized by a linear progression from requirements gathering to design to implementation to testing. In contrast, the Agile approach is more iterative and incremental, with developers working in short cycles (called sprints) to deliver new features or functionality. Organizations that adopt an Agile approach to software development typically do so in order to increase flexibility and responsiveness to change. The Agile approach is well-suited for projects that are subject to frequent changes or where requirements are not well-defined at the outset. There are many different flavors of Agile methodology, but all share some common principles, including a focus on collaboration, customer satisfaction, and continuous improvement.

Agile methodology has been shown to be an effective approach to software development, and many organizations have successfully adopted this approach. However, it is important to note that no single methodology is right for every organization or every project. Each organization should select the approach that makes the most sense for their specific needs (Ashmore & Runyan, 2014).

2.2.2. Agile Mindset of the Organization

An Agile mindset is essential for any organization that wants to stay ahead of the competition. The Agile methodology has taken the business world by storm, and for good reason. This iterative and incremental approach to software development is perfect for organizations that need to be able to rapidly respond to change.

The Agile methodology has been adopted by organizations of all sizes, in all industries. That is because the benefits of Agile are hard to ignore. Organizations that use the Agile approach are able to deliver software faster, with fewer defects. They are also able to better respond to changes in customer needs. It is important to understand that Agile is not a one-size-fits-all solution. There is no "right way" to do Agile – instead, each organization needs to find what works best for them. It is also important to have buy-in from all members of the organization. Agile will only be successful if everyone is on board and committed to making it work. Finally, it is important to remember that Agile is an ongoing journey, not a destination. There is always room for improvement, and the best

Agile organizations are always learning and evolving (Manen & Vliet, 2014).

2.2.3. Agile Mindset of an Agile Leader

Some of the challenges that can occur during an Agile implementation include:

1) Employee resistance to change.
2) Lack of understanding of Agile methods.
3) Implementation failures due to inadequate planning.
4) Inadequate resources or support from upper management.
5) Unrealistic expectations about the results of the transition.

By being aware of these challenges, leaders can be prepared to address them if they arise. Additionally, they can take steps to prevent or mitigate these challenges.

Some tips for leaders during an Agile implementation include:

1) Communicate the vision and objectives for the transition to all employees.
2) Create a dedicated team responsible for overseeing the transition.
3) Train all employees in the basics of Agile methods.
4) Implement Agile methods incrementally, starting with small projects.
5) Monitor progress closely and make adjustments as needed.

Below table describes the mindset and behavioral shifts required for Agile Leaders.

Table 2. 2 Mindset and Behavioral Shifts for Agile Leader

Agile Leader	
Mindset	**Behavioral Shifts**
Innovation and Value Creation	Focus on customer satisfaction
Experimentation	Empowers and coaches teams towards risk-taking and self-direction
Continuous Learning	Creates an environment of trust and support
Excellence	Leads teams towards continuous improvement
Collaboration	Collaborates across boundaries
Positive Relationship	Demonstrates empathy with customers and teams
Growth	Leads teams towards continuous learning

Source: Anonymous (n.d.)

With this mindset and behavioral shifts, leaders can increase the likelihood of a successful Agile adoption. In turn, this can lead to a number of benefits for the organization, its employees, and its customers (Moreira, 2013).

2.2.4. Agile Management Style

On a conventional project, a manager might actively participate in assigning tasks to the team and directing their work. This is also known as command and control. The manager's function in Agile management is primarily that of a facilitator, and it is to make sure that the company and the developers are working together effectively (Carroll, 2012. p14).

2.2.5. Culture of Agile Organization

There are several Agile methodologies and all share a common set of values and principles. These include a focus on individuals and interactions over process and tools; working software over comprehensive documentation; customer collaboration over contract negotiation; and responding to change over following a plan. In an Agile organization, everyone is responsible for the success of the project. There is no need for formal roles like "Project Manager" or "Scrum Master." Instead, team members take on whatever tasks are necessary to get the job done. This often leads to more creativity and innovation, as team members are free to experiment and explore new ideas. Advocates of the Agile methodology contend that corporate culture affects how widely the methodology is applied (Strode, Huff & Tretiakov, 2009).

Agile methodology also values transparency and communication. All stakeholders should have a clear understanding of the project's goals, progress, and risks. This transparency helps to build trust between the team and stakeholders. The Agile approach can be applied to any type of project, from software development to marketing campaigns. It is particularly well-suited for projects that are likely to experience changes or uncertainties. For companies going to adopt Agile Methodologies, first, it is important to have buy-in from all stakeholders. Second, you will need to be prepared to embrace change and adapt your plans accordingly. And finally, remember that communication is key to success. With the right mindset and preparation, you can leverage the power of Agile methodology to achieve amazing results (Shore & Warden, 2021).

2.3. Agile Design & Architecture

Agile design is a methodology that values customer collaboration and feedback, iterative development, and working software above all else. In Agile design & architecture, requirements are constantly changing and evolving as new information comes to light, so the focus is on building software that can adapt to these changes quickly and easily. This means simplify code and designs, writing tests early and often, and automating as much of the process as possible. The Agile design & architecture process usually starts with a very high-level overview of what the final product should do. From there, the team works together to break down the project into smaller pieces that can be completed in short iterations (usually two weeks or less). Each iteration starts with a planning meeting where the team decides which features to work on next. Then they design, build, test, and deploy the new code. At the end of each iteration, there is a review meeting where the team discusses what things went well and what things could be improved (Ferreira, Noble, & Biddle, 2007).

Figure 2. 3 Agile Design

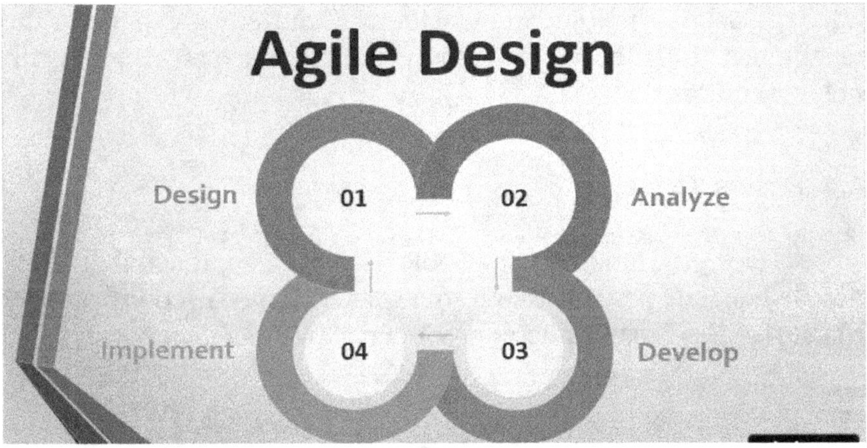

source: www.educba.com

As shown in the above figure, Agile Design & architecture is an iterative process, starts with design, analyze, develop & implement.

There are many reasons why Agile design has become so popular in recent years. First and foremost, it helps teams move faster and adapt to change more easily. By breaking down projects into smaller pieces and delivering working software frequently, Agile teams can make changes quickly and easily without having to start from scratch each time. Additionally, Agile design & architecture forces teams to focus on customer feedback and collaboration. This ensures that the final product is something that customers actually want and need, instead of something that the team thinks they want. First, it is important to have a clear vision for what you want to build. This will help the team focus on the most important features and avoid scope creep. Second, you need to be prepared to change course based on feedback from customers and users. Agile design & architecture is all about being flexible and adapting to change, so do not be afraid to pivot if necessary. Finally, make sure you have a good toolset in place. Agile teams need tools that help them manage their work, collaborate effectively, and automate repetitive tasks (Pereira & de FSM Russo, 2018).

Design Thinking and Customer Centricity are some of the techniques of Agile Design & Architecture, which are described in below sections.

2.4. Design Thinking

Design Thinking is a problem-solving approach that helps people generate new ideas and solutions. It can be used in a variety of settings, such as business, product development, and design.

Figure 2. 4 Design Thinking

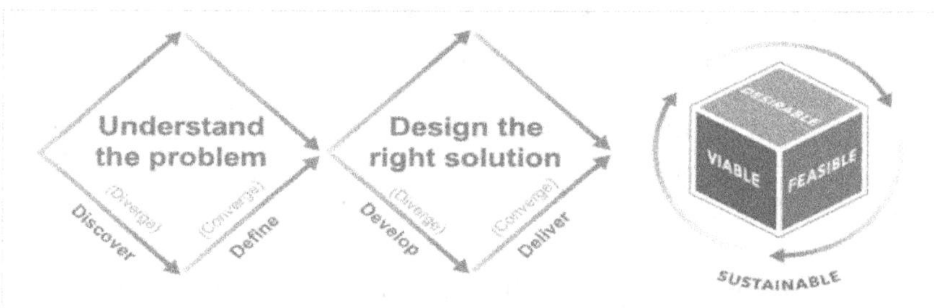

Source: www.scaledAgileframework.com

Design thinking begins with understanding the problem that needs to be solved. This can involve researching the topic, talking to experts, and doing user research. Next, designers generate ideas for solving the problem. These ideas can be sketched out or turned into prototypes. After testing and refining the prototypes, the best solution is chosen and implemented (Razzouk & Shute, 2012).

2.5. Customer Centricity

Customer centricity is a way of thinking and operating that puts the customer at the center of the whole range of goods and services that the company provides. Businesses that focus on their consumers make more money, engage their workforce more, and have happier customers. Governments and charitable organizations that focus on their customers provide the resilience, sustainability, and alignment necessary to accomplish their goals. Delivering whole-product solutions that are created with a thorough grasp of client demands is a hallmark of all customer-centric businesses (Fader, 2020).

Empathetic design is used throughout the design process in customer-centric businesses. The capacity to set aside our preconceived notions and create solutions from the perspective of our clients is referred to as empathic design. Teams are motivated by empathic design to comprehend and experience the world from the viewpoint of the customer, learning about and appreciating the challenges they encounter, their responsibilities, and their work setting. It places a focus on user research and includes actions like Gemba walks (visiting the place where the customer work is done). Gemba fosters empathy by assisting Agile teams to better comprehend the user's emotional and physical needs—the way they see, comprehend, and engage with their environment.

Figure 2. 5 Customer Centricity

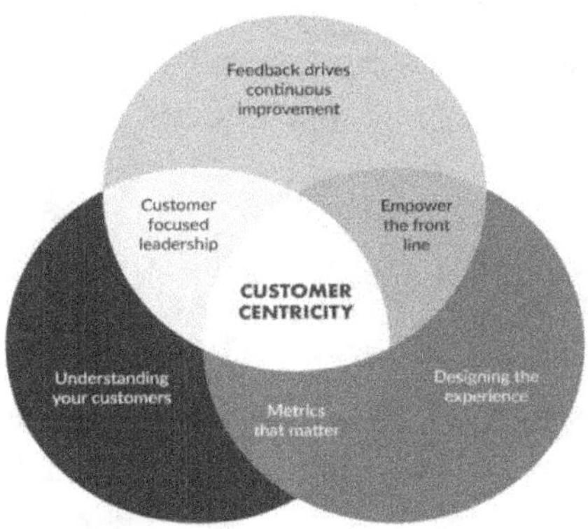

Source: www.superoffice.com

In order to be customer-centric, organizations need to have Agile frameworks in place that allow for quick and flexible response to changing customer needs. The most popular Agile framework is Scrum, which is an iterative and incremental approach to software development that focus on customer satisfaction by giving customers useful software early and often. Other popular Agile frameworks include Kanban and Lean (Fader, 2020).

2.6. Agile Implementation

According to Livermore (2008), Agile methodologies provide a framework for managing complex projects in a targeted manner. It focuses on speed, scalability, and customer feedback to ensure the successful delivery of projects. In order to successfully implement an Agile methodology, there are certain techniques that can be used.

One common technique is the use of cross-functional teams. By having members of the team work on different aspects of a project, it allows ideas and solutions to be developed quickly. This also creates an environment of collaboration and innovation as team members are able to learn from each other and share best practices.

Another technique is the use of sprints. Sprints allow for rapid iteration and testing, allowing teams to quickly adapt to customer feedback and make changes as needed. This ensures that the final product is of high quality, meeting customer requirements and expectations.

The practice of continuous integration (CI) is also part of Agile implementation. CI allows for automated testing and deployment, allowing for faster release cycles and improved overall project visibility. It also encourages teams to work together and collaborate, as all changes are integrated into the same codebase.

Finally, to ensure a successful Agile implementation, teams must have a clear understanding of their project goals. Each team member should understand their role in meeting these objectives and how they fit within the overall process. This helps everyone align on project requirements, making it easier to prioritize tasks and ensure timely delivery.

2.6.1. Strategy to Implement Agility

There are four primary components to an Agile strategy: people, process, technology, and metrics, detailed below (Mathiassen & Pries-Heje, 2006).

1) **People:** The people component of an Agile strategy refers to the team that will be implementing the Agile methodology. This team should be cross-functional, with members from different departments who can bring a variety of skills and perspectives to the table.
2) **Process:** The process component of an Agile strategy outlines how the team will go about implementing the methodology. This includes defining what tasks need to be completed, how they will be completed, and who is responsible for each task.
3) **Technology:** The technology component of an Agile strategy defines what tools and systems will be used to support the implementation of the methodology. This includes everything from project management software to communication tools.
4) **Metrics:** The metrics component of an Agile strategy defines how the team will measure success. This includes setting targets for how much work should be completed in each iteration and how often the team should review their progress.

An Agile strategy is not complete without all four of these components. People, process, technology, and metrics all need to be considered in order to create a successful Agile transformation.

2.6.1.1. Agile Project Roadmap

Carroll (2012) designed Agile Project Roadmap with following phases: Pre-project, Feasibility, Foundations, Exploration, Engineering, Deployment, and post project.

These phases are shown in the below figure and details are described for each phase.

Figure 2. 6 Agile Project Roadmap

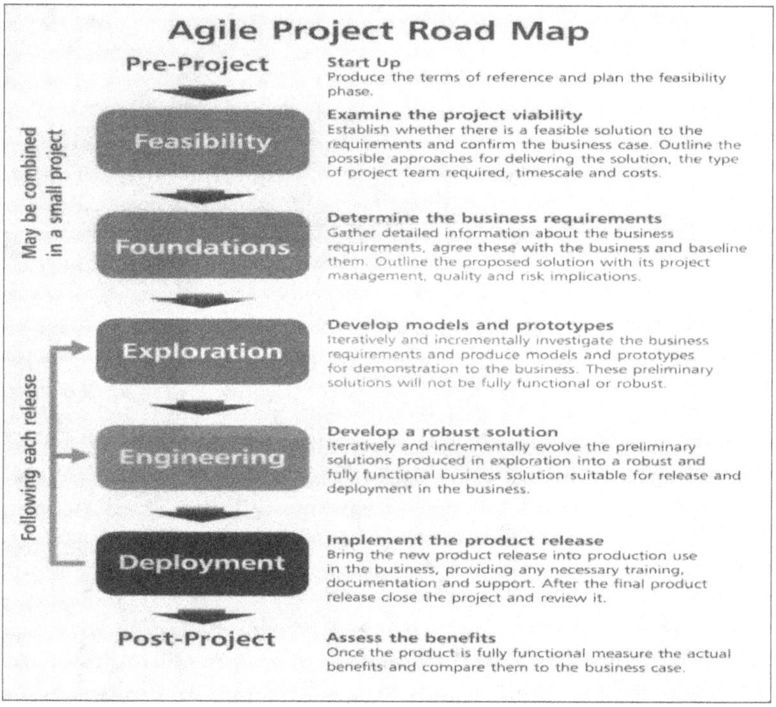

Source: Carroll (2012)

Pre-project: This is a startup phase where terms of reference produced and plan is produced.

Feasibility: In the feasibility phase of an Agile project, it is important to decide if the project is actually feasible or not. You should analyze factors such as how long will it take to complete, what resources are needed, and how much effort would be required for the project.

Foundations: After determining if your project is feasible, should include the scope of the project (high-level and low-level requirements), timeline, resources needed, cost and risk assessment. An important factor to consider during this stage is how you will track progress throughout the project.

Exploration: During the exploration stage, you should explore possible solutions to your project. You should also define user stories and create wireframes or prototypes if needed.

Engineering/Development: This is where the actual development of your project takes place. This might include coding a website or app, designing user interfaces, creating databases, etc. It is important to use Agile techniques such as pair programming and test-driven development to ensure quality. Once the development is completed, solution need to be tested to make sure it is working as expected. This should include unit testing and user acceptance testing. Setting up a test environment can help with this.

Deployment: After everything is tested and approved, the project can be deployed. This should involve setting up the production environment and making sure everything is in place before going live.

Maintenance/Post-project: Finally, once your project has been successfully deployed, you need to monitor it over time and make any necessary changes or updates to ensure optimal performance. This is an ongoing process that should be done on a regular basis.

By following these Agile project roadmap steps, an effective Agile project implementation goes smoothly and stays on track.

2.6.1.2. Agile Canvas

Agile Canvas is an approach to business planning that is based on the Agile software development methodology. The Agile canvas is a tool that helps teams to be more flexible and adaptable in their work. It is a way of working that breaks down projects into smaller pieces, so that they can be completed more quickly and with less risk (Link & Lewrick, 2014).

Figure 2. 7 Agile Project Canvas

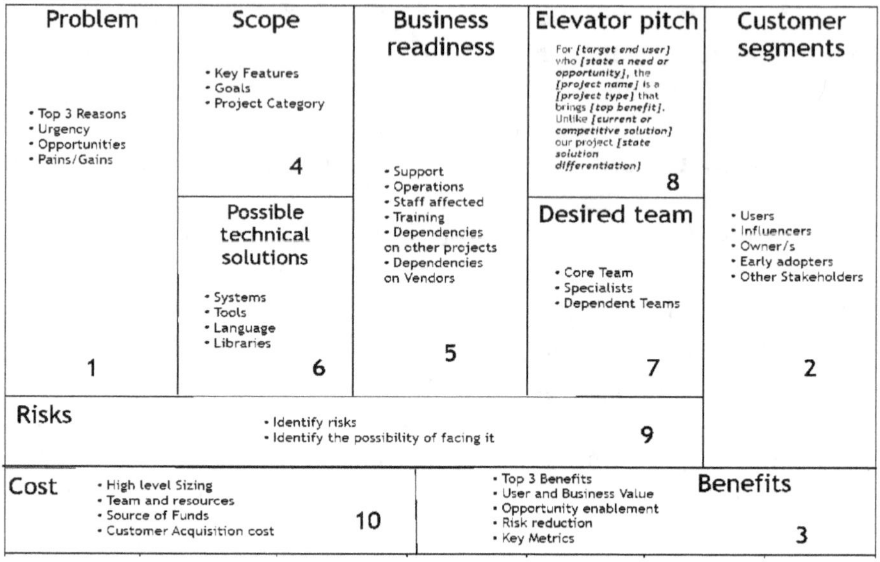

Source: https://thecanvasrevolution.com/product/Agile-project-canvas

The Agile canvas is based on the principle of iterative development, which means that tasks are divided into small, manageable chunks and then completed one at a time. This approach allows for quick feedback and changes to be made along the way, so that the final product is more likely to meet the needs of the customer. The Agile canvas is a valuable tool for businesses that want to create a flexible and adaptable business plan (Link & Lewrick, 2014).

2.6.1.3. Steps in Agile Implementation

The major steps in Agile Implementation include:

Agile Planning: Agile planning focuses on mapping out the process and tasks required to reach the desired outcome. This means that each step is carefully considered, and any potential challenges that may arise during execution are taken into account. It also involves breaking down a project into smaller pieces, so that progress can be tracked and any changes or delays in one area can be easily identified. This level of detail ensures that the team is able to stay on track and everyone involved understands the overall goal (Cohn, 2005).

Agile Execution: Once a plan has been created, it is time to begin execution. This involves assigning tasks and setting deadlines for each step in the process. Agile methods employ an iterative approach, which means that each part of the project is tested, adjusted if necessary, and then integrated into the whole. This approach allows teams to stay on track while still being flexible enough to respond to changes in scope or timing (Sarangee, et al, 2022).

Agile Monitoring: The monitoring process ensures that all aspects of the project are functioning as intended, and that overall progress is being made towards the goal. This involves regularly assessing progress against the plan, ensuring that any risks have been identified and addressed, and keeping stakeholders informed of progress. It also allows teams to identify areas where improvements can be made in order to speed up completion or increase quality. Regular monitoring helps teams stay on track by allowing them to quickly address issues before they become major problems (Miranda & Bourque, 2010).

Agile Reporting: Agile reporting is a vital part of the implementation process, as it allows teams to track progress and ensure they are meeting their commitments. Reports provide an overview of the project, including milestones achieved, tasks yet to be completed, risks identified and mitigation strategies implemented. They also help stakeholders stay informed by providing a detailed picture of the project's progress (Cooke, 2012).

Agile Adaptation: The final step in Agile implementation is adaptation. This means that teams need to be prepared to make changes as needed in order to stay on track and meet their goals. It also involves adjusting the plan based on feedback from stakeholders, ensuring that any new information or requests are taken into account. Agile methods are designed to be adaptive, so that teams can respond quickly and effectively to changing circumstances (Venkatesh & Rakhra, 2020).

2.6.1.4. Agile Playbook

The Agile playbook is an important tool for any organization undergoing an Agile transformation. The playbook can help ensure that everyone is on the same page with respect to the Agile process, and it can help keep the transformation on track. The playbook should be updated regularly to reflect the progress of the transformation, and it should be tailored to the specific needs of the organization (Küng, 2017).

The Agile Playbook provides a framework for organizations to follow during an Agile transformation. This includes specifying the roles and responsibilities of each team member, outlining the processes that will be used, and detailing how progress will be tracked. The playbook also includes best practices for implementing Agile methodology, such as using iterative development and continuous integration (Küng, 2017).

Thc Agile Playbook is constantly evolving as new best practices are discovered. As such, it is important for organizations to regularly review and update their playbook. Doing so will help ensure that the Agile transformation is successful and that the organization is able to realize the full benefits of Agile methodology (Küng, 2017).

There are a number of resources available to help organizations create and maintain their Agile Playbook. The Scrum Alliance, for example, offers a free online course that covers the basics of creating an Agile transformation roadmap. Additionally, a number of books and articles have been published on the topic of Agile playbooks, and these can be helpful in understanding how to tailor the playbook to the specific needs of an organization (Küng, 2017).

2.6.2. How to Choose Suitable Agile Frameworks

When it comes to choosing an Agile framework, there are a few popular ones that are often recommended. These include Scrum, Kanban, and XP. However, the best one to choose will depend on the specific needs of your project (Rasnacis, & Berzisa, 2017).

Some factors to consider when choosing an Agile framework include:

- The size and complexity of the project
- The team's experience with Agile methods
- The team's preferences
- The business context

Before selecting a framework, it is important to understand your team's needs and what you are trying to achieve. Each framework has its own set of practices and rituals that need to be followed in order to be effective.

Adapted Stacy Matrix

The Stacy matrix is a tool used to visualize risks associated with various activities. It is based on the work of Robert C. Stacy, an early pioneer in risk management. Maretzke (2019) suggests using Stacey Matrix to choose an Agile method. Software projects often fail. Late, over budget, or no corporate value. Agile approaches are often blamed for software development failures. Life is often gray. Context determines best software process method. I combined industry feedback on Agile vs. traditional software development methods.

Figure 2. 8 Adapted Stacey Matrix

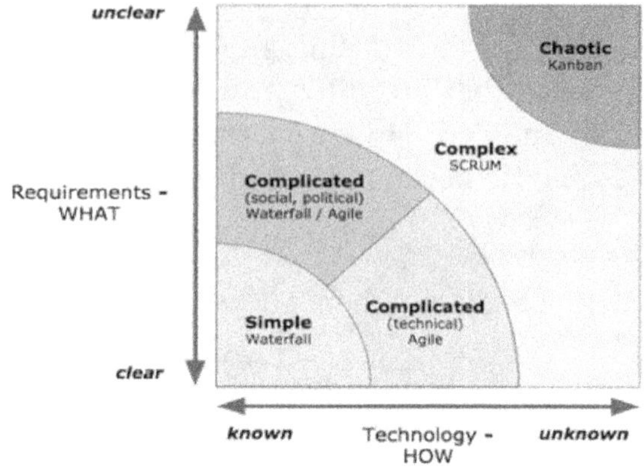

Simple	Complicated	Complex	Chaotic
Waterfall	Waterfall / Agile	SCRUM	Kanban
Known Knowns	*Known Unknowns*	*Unknown Unknowns*	*Unknowables*
Routine	Domain of experts	No previous experience	No recognizable patterns
Sense - Categorize - Respond	Sense - Analyze - Respond	Probe - Sense - Respond	Act - Sense - Respond

From knowns to unknowns

Source: https://www.Agile-minds.com/when-to-use-waterfall-when-Agile/

The original Stacey matrix offers appropriate management measures for simple, complex, chaotic, and convoluted scenarios. Decision context has a significant impact on suggested actions. Adapted Stacey matrix dimensions: HOW and WHAT. By using the adapted Stacy matrix, organizations can not only get a better view of current risk levels but also anticipate future risks as changes occur within their operations. It can be used to identify and assess unknown risks, helping organizations put the necessary measures in place to effectively manage any potential losses that may result. The matrix also provides insights into areas where rewards are greater but associated risks are lower, allowing businesses to take advantage of these opportunities without putting themselves at undue risk. It is possible to choose suitable methodology based on the following risk categories: *Simple = known knowns*, *Complicated = not simple but known unknowns*,

Complex = not entirely known but somewhat predictable and *Chaos = unknowables* (Bizjack, 2021; Maretzke, 2019)

Overall, the Stacy matrix is an invaluable tool for any organization looking to assess risk, identify opportunities, and determine the best course of action. By utilizing the matrix, organizations can ensure that their operations remain well-managed and profitable over time (Bizjack, 2021).

2.6.3. Success factors for Implementing Agile

There are a number of success factors to consider when implementing an Agile methodology within an organization. The following discusses some of the most important ones (Misra, Kumar, & Kumar, 2006):

- **Clear and concise communication** - all members of the team need to be on the same page in regards to objectives, goals, and expectations. This can be achieved through regular stand-up meetings, task trackers, and other forms of communication.
- **Cross-functional teams** - it is important to have teams that are cross-functional, meaning they have all the skills necessary to complete the project at hand. This helps to avoid dependencies and ensures that work can flow smoothly.
- **Self-organizing teams** - another key success factor is for teams to be self-organizing. This means that they are able to prioritize and assign tasks based on the needs of the project.
- **Iterative and incremental approach** - an Agile methodology is all about taking an iterative and incremental approach to development. This means that work is done in small increments so that it can be easily tested and feedback can be gathered along the way.
- **Flexibility** - finally, it is important to be flexible when implementing an Agile methodology. Things will inevitably change throughout the course of a project and it is important to be able to adapt accordingly.

By keeping these success factors in mind, organizations can increase their chances of successfully implementing an Agile methodology.

2.6.4. Ways to Increase Transparency

Agile Transparency is a key part of Agile Implementation. It emphasizes openness and teamwork in the workplace by encouraging everyone to collaborate, communicate, and share information. Transparency promotes trust and accountability, creating a more effective and successful working environment. This transparency is further enabled through team-based decision making, allowing everyone to contribute their skillset and expertise to the project. Some of the ways to increase transparency in Agile methodology include (Betta & Boronina, 2018):

- ✓ Regular stand-up meetings
- ✓ Iterative and incremental development
- ✓ Continuous integration
- ✓ Test-driven development or behavior-driven development

2.6.5. Ways to Increase Velocity

Agile Velocity is a key performance indicator for tracking the progress of Agile implementation. It measures the amount of work completed in a single iteration, typically measured in points per hour. This metric can provide visibility into both the speed and quality of development, as well as overall project progress. Agile Velocity also helps identify risks early on and potential areas for improvement, allowing teams to make adjustments as needed (Omanovic & Buza, 2013).

- ➢ **Continuous Delivery**: Make sure that code is always in a deployable state. This means automating as much of the build, testing, and deployment process as possible.
- ➢ **Feature Branches**: Develop features on their own branches and merge them into the main development branch when they

are done. This allows developers to work on features in parallel without impacting each other's code.

- **Automated Testing**: Automate as much of the testing process as possible. This includes unit tests, integration tests, regression tests, etc.
- **Code Reviews**: Conduct regular code reviews to ensure that code quality remains high and that everyone is on the same page regarding implementation details.
- **Refactoring**: Always be prepared to refactor code as necessary. This includes extracting methods, creating new classes, etc.

Increasing the velocity of development can be difficult, but it is important to remember that small changes can have a big impact. If you adopt even just one or two of these practices, you should see a significant improvement in your team's ability to deliver features quickly and efficiently.

2.6.6. Self-Management and Relation of it to Agility

Self-management is a key principle of Agile methodology. It is based on the idea that teams are better equipped to manage themselves and their work, than managers are. This empowers team members to make decisions and take responsibility for their own work. Self-management also promotes transparency and collaboration within teams. By sharing information openly and working together, team members can more effectively solve problems and meet deadlines (Gutierrez, et al., 2018).

The benefits of self-management include:

- **Increased Efficiency:** Teams that self-manage are able to move faster and be more productive.
- **Improved Quality:** When team members have a say in how their work is done, they are more likely to do it well.
- **Greater Satisfaction:** Team members who feel empowered and respected are more likely to be satisfied with their work.

➢ **Improved Retention:** When employees feel like they have a stake in their work, they are more likely to stay with the company.

Self-management is not without any challenges, however, one of the biggest challenges is ensuring that everyone on the team is on the same page. Without clear guidelines and expectations, teams can quickly become chaotic and unproductive. Another challenge is dealing with team members who are not comfortable with taking responsibility for their own work. These team members may need more time to adjust to the new way of working.

2.7. Digital Transformation

The term digital transformation refers to the process by which a company integrates digital technology into every aspect of its operations. This leads to significant shifts in the ways in which companies function and the ways in which they provide value to their consumers. As our world becomes increasingly digitized, businesses must find ways to keep up with the pace of change or risk being left behind. Digital transformation is not just about adopting new technologies; it is about using those technologies to create new or optimized business processes, products, and services that drive growth and competitive advantage. In other words, it is about using technology to create value for your business and your customers (Ebert & Duarte, 2018).

By definition, digital transformation is a strategic change initiative that enables organizations to leverage digital technologies to create new or improved business processes, products, and services that drive value and competitive advantage. Digital transformation requires a holistic approach that takes into account people, process, and technology. To be successful, businesses must start with a clear understanding of their customers and what they need or want. They also need to have the right processes in place to support the new digital initiatives. And finally, they need to adopt the right technologies to enable those initiatives.

Technology is just one piece of the digital transformation puzzle; it is not an end in itself. The goal is to use technology to create new or optimized business processes, products, and services that drive value and competitive advantage. As digital technologies continue to evolve, businesses must continually adapt their strategies to stay ahead of the curve. In the 21st century, digital transformation is key to business success. Those who can move quickly and adapt to change will be the winners. In order to achieve agility in digital transformation, businesses need to have the following:

1) A clear vision and strategy
2) The right people in place
3) The ability to execute quickly
4) A culture of innovation
5) A focus on customer experience
6) The use of technology as a driver for change
7) A willingness to experiment and learn from failures
8) A focus on continual improvement
9) An Agile mindset throughout the organization
10) The right partners and suppliers
11) The right tools and processes in place
12) A willingness to embrace change
13) A focus on results
14) A commitment to excellence
15) A positive attitude

Following the above steps will help the businesses help in going in the right directions towards digital transformation. Digital transformation is a journey, not a destination. It is an ongoing process that requires continual evolution and adaptation.

2.8. Agility in Digital Transformation

Agile become popular approach for many organizations undertaking digital transformation initiatives. Agile methodology focuses on delivering value to the customer through rapid iterations. This allows organizations to get feedback early and often, which helps them make course corrections as needed. Organizations that adopt Agile methods for their digital transformation journey typically see increased efficiency, quality, and customer satisfaction. Additionally, Agile approaches help reduce risks associated with traditional waterfall methods (Schlömer, 2022).

2.9. Popular Change Models for Agile Transformation

There are a number of change models that can be used in Agile transformations, which are described below.

2.9.1. The Lewin's Change Model

Lewin's change model is one such change model. The model consists of three stages: unfreezing, changing, and refreezing. In the unfreezing stage, the team prepares for change by recognizing that there is a need for change and that things cannot stay the same. In the changing stage, the team actually makes the changes. In the refreezing stage, the team ensures that the changes are sustainable by reinforcing the new behaviors and norms (Levasseur, 2001).

Figure 2. 9 Lewin's Change Management Model

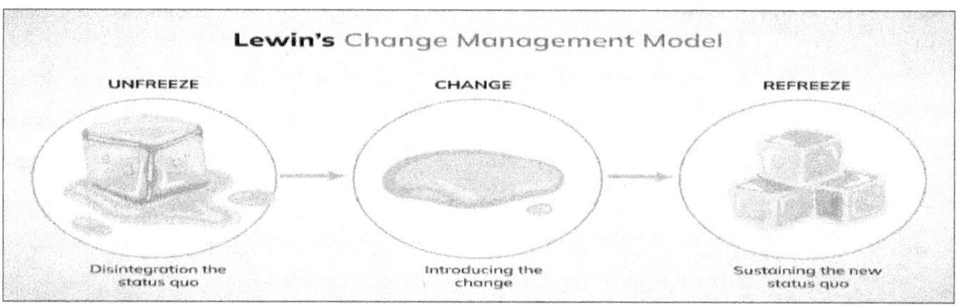

Source: www.crowjack.com

2.9.2. Six Box Model

The Marvin Weisberg Six Box Model is an organizational development model named after the psychologist Marvin

Weisberg. It provides a framework for understanding the relationship between an organization's activities and how it can best achieve its goals. The six boxes of the model are: environment, strategy, structure, processes, people and culture (Ihsani & Syuhada, 2020).

The **environment** box represents both internal and external factors that influence an organization's decision-making. This includes things like market trends, customer feedback and competitive forces. By considering these elements when making decisions about how to move forward, an organization can ensure that its strategy aligns with current needs and realities in its sector or industry.

Strategy involves setting clear goals and then creating a plan of action to reach those objectives. This box also covers developing the right tools and resources to help make progress towards those goals. Strategy must be regularly revisited to ensure that it reflects any changes in the environment surrounding the organization.

Structure refers to how an organization organizes itself internally. This encompasses things like job design, division of roles and responsibilities, team formations and reporting structures. All of these aspects are key in helping an organization create effective communication channels within itself as well as maintain alignment between different divisional goals.

Processes refer to how tasks get completed within the organization from start to finish. These may include standard procedures or even more specific steps for individual projects or initiatives undertaken by the company - all with the aim of ensuring that outcomes are achieved efficiently and effectively within a reasonable timeframe.

People refer to all stakeholders involved in achieving organizational outcomes - from employees working on projects on a daily basis to senior management setting out overall direction for the business, each individual plays a key role in driving success for any given initiative or goal set by an organization.

Finally, **culture** refers to shared beliefs, values, attitudes and behaviors that characterize workplace relationships among individuals within an organization as well as between employees across different departments or divisions of a company. A strong corporate culture can help foster collaboration while also providing guidance on how teams work together to achieve desired results more efficiently than if they worked independently of one another's efforts.

The Marvin Weisberg Six Box Model helps provide a holistic view of how an organization functions and can be used as a tool to identify areas for improvement or change. By taking into consideration all six boxes when making decisions, organizations can ensure that their activities are purpose driven and are ultimately aligned with their overall goals. The six-box model is a popular way to visualize the Agile transformation process. It divides the transformation process into six steps (Ihsani & Syuhada, 2020):

1. Pre-Transformation: This is where the organization is before it begins its Agile journey
2. Initiation: This is where the organization decides to embark on an Agile journey and lays out the initial plan
3. Formation: This is where the organization starts to change its processes and culture to be more Agile
4. Storming: This is where the organization begins to experience turbulence as it changes its ways
5. Norming: This is where the organization settles into its new Agile ways and begins to reap the benefits of being Agile
6. Performing: This is where the organization becomes a high-performing Agile organization.

These steps help organizations in successful Agile transformation.

2.9.3. The Kotter Eight Step Plan

The Kotter Eight Step Plan is an effective means of introducing change into your organization, ensuring that all employees understand and are invested in the process. With a well-thought-out plan, the implementation of change can be successful and sustainable in the long term (Spencer & Winn, 2005).

This plan provides a roadmap for implementing change in an organized and methodical way. It starts by creating a sense of urgency, then moves on to forming a powerful guiding coalition, developing a vision and strategies, communicating the change vision, empowering employees to act on the vision, generating short-term wins along the way, consolidating improvements, and anchoring the changes in the organizational culture.

This plan provides a roadmap for implementing change successfully in any organization. It is based on over 35 years of research and has been used by organizations around the world. The eight steps are: 1) Establish a sense of urgency, 2) Create a coalition of supporters, 3) Develop a vision and strategy, 4) Communicate the vision, 5) Empower employees, 6) Enable action, 7) Reinforce new behavior, 8) Sustain momentum (Spencer & Winn, 2005).

2.9.4. The Greiner Model

The Greiner Model is a business model that was introduced by John Greiner in the late 1970s. This model provides organizations with an effective way to structure their processes, products and services for efficient operations. It focuses on identifying and understanding the core elements of a business in order to make well-informed decisions about how it should be organized and managed. The model consists of five stages: Initiate, Create and Manage, Grow, Expand and Mature. Each stage has its own set of challenges that must be addressed in order to move on to the next stage. By successfully navigating each stage, organizations can ensure their future success. This model is widely used by businesses around the world as part of their strategic planning process. It enables organizations to develop and implement strategies that will help them reach their desired goals. With the Greiner Model, businesses can ensure that they are well-prepared for any unpredictable changes in the market and can adjust accordingly. As such, this model is a helpful tool in understanding an organization's current position and how to move forward (Mulder, 2013).

2.9.5. Cumming and Worley Model

The Cumming and Worley Model is a research model developed by Clive R.W. Cumming and Philip C. Worley in the late 1960s. The main aim of this model is to help researchers understand the complexities of organizational behavior, particularly how organizations respond to changes in their environment and how decisions are made within them (Cummings & Worley, 2014).

The model is made up of four distinct components: the environment, organizations, decision-making processes, and behavior. It is based on a systems approach to understanding organizational behavior which takes into account the interactions between different elements within an organization. The model provides a framework for analyzing the environment in which organizations operate and how they respond to changes in that environment. It also considers how decisions are made within organizations and the impact of these decisions on organizational behavior. The model helps researchers to examine how an organization reacts to external forces, such as competition or government regulations, and internal forces like worker morale or organizational structure.

2.9.6. Burke and Littwak Model

The Burke and Littwak Model, also known as the Optimal Strategy Model, is an influential framework used to analyze strategic decision making in business and government contexts. Developed by John R. Burke and Mark Littwak in 1983, this model offers a systematic approach to analyzing decisions that are made under conditions of uncertainty. It considers the effect of a decision's consequences on all involved parties and allows managers to compare alternative strategies based on their expected returns.

The model is based on the idea that firms and organizations should maximize their output given limited resources, while minimizing potential losses or other unforeseen risks. In order to do this effectively, it requires that they evaluate all possible outcomes and make optimal decisions based on their expected returns. The model thus allows managers to compare different strategies and identify the one that will yield the best results for the particular context in which it is applied. This is especially important when making decisions with multiple stakeholders, as each stakeholder's interests must be taken into consideration (Burke & Litwin, 1992).

2.9.7. John Fisher Change Model

The John Fisher Change Model is a six-step process designed to help individuals and organizations move through change in a way that is beneficial for everyone involved. It was developed by organizational psychologist, John P. Fisher, who believed that successful implementation of change requires active involvement from all stakeholders (Fisher, 2005).

At the heart of the model are three key elements:
1. **Unfreezing** – This step involves creating space for change by challenging existing beliefs and behaviors. It can be achieved through the use of reflection, dialogue, and brainstorming.
2. **Moving** – Here individuals or teams discuss how to create new processes that will realize the desired outcome. A number of problem-solving techniques can be used to come up with creative solutions.

3. **Refreezing** – This stage is where the new behaviors and beliefs are tested and reinforced through practice, monitoring, and feedback. This helps to ensure that the change sticks in the long term.

The John Fisher Change Model encourages individuals and organizations to approach change in a methodical and collaborative way. By following the steps outlined in the model, it is possible to create positive and lasting change that will benefit all stakeholders.

2.10. Management 3.0 and Agile

Management 3.0 is an approach to management that is based on Agile principles. It emphasizes collaboration, communication, and feedback loops between managers and employees. It also aims to create an environment where employees are empowered to make decisions and take ownership of their work.

Management 3.0 is complementary to Agile because it helps to build a better foundation for Agile teams by focusing on the management aspects of product development. It provides a clear framework and set of practices for managing product development, which can help to ensure that Agile teams are able to operate effectively and efficiently. One of the key benefits of Management 3.0 is that it helps to promote collaboration and communication between all members of the product development team. This is essential for Agile teams, as it helps to ensure that everyone is working towards the same goal and that ideas can be freely shared without fear of conflict or misunderstanding.

Another benefit of Management 3.0 is that it helps to encourage experimentation and innovation. This is again crucial for Agile teams, as it allows them to try new things and learn from their mistakes in order to continuously improve their process. Overall, Management 3.0 provides a solid foundation for Agile teams to work from, and its focus on collaboration, communication, and innovation can help to make sure that Agile teams are able to operate at their best. (Almeida, Oliveira & Neves, 2022)

According to Masgo (2021), the 5 principles of Management 3.0 include: Engaging the people and their interactions, improving the system, help delight all the clients, manage the system and not the people, and finally co create the work.

2.11. Management 4.0

Management 4.0 is a term that has been coined to describe the current trend of using Agile methodology in the workplace. Agile methodology is a way of organizing and managing work that is focused on delivering value to the customer quickly and efficiently. It relies on teamwork, communication, and collaboration, and can be used in a variety of industries and businesses. The term "Management 4.0" was first coined by German software engineer and management consultant Frank Schiller in 2010. In his book "Management 4.0: Leading Agile Developers, Developing Agile Leaders", Schiller (2010) argues that the conventional top-down approach to management is no longer effective in today's fast-paced, globalized world. He advocates for a more Agile, decentralized approach that empowers employees and encourages innovation. Since the inception of the concept of Management 4.0, it has been gaining popularity worldwide. Many businesses have adopted Agile methodology in order to stay competitive and deliver value to their customers (Haleem et al., 2022).

2.12. DevOps

In contrast to conventional software development and infrastructure management techniques, DevOps is a set of cultural concepts, procedures, and technological advancements that improve an organization's capacity to create software and services. As a result, products can be developed and improved more quickly.

Because of its effectiveness, businesses may enhance their offerings and keep a competitive edge. DevOps is founded on three key tenets (López Martín de Blas, n.d.):

1. **Continuous integration (CI)**: is concerned with assembling the work of various developers into a repository. Every time a code submission is made, it is automatically built, tested, and any bugs are found right away.
2. **Continuous deployment (CD):** The process from code to production is automated and streamlined if the CI and CD tests are successful.
3. **Continuous Learning & Monitoring:** When clients are prepared to use the CI, CD, and monitoring tools, innovations are given to them during the third phase of continuous learning and monitoring. (López Martín de Blas, n.d.)

Companies should focus on the above principles for effective results and be ahead of its competition.

2.13. DevSecOps

DevSecOps is a term that is used to describe the integration of security into the development processes. It includes the use of automation and other tools to help secure the software development process. DevSecOps helps to ensure that security is considered throughout the entire software development life cycle, from planning and design through to testing and deployment.

DevSecOps is an important part of the Agile methodology, as it helps to avoid security vulnerabilities that can be introduced during development. It also helps to ensure that security is considered throughout the entire project, from start to finish. By integrating security into the development process, DevSecOps can help to improve the overall security of a software application. DevSecOps is complementary to Agile because it helps to ensure that security is integrated into the development process. This helps to avoid security vulnerabilities that can be introduced during development and ensures that security is considered throughout the entire project (Tomas, Li & Huang, 2019).

2.14. Business Transformation

Business transformation is the process of aligning an organization's strategy, processes, people and technology to create a more efficient and effective organization. It can be done in response to changes in the external environment, such as new regulations, or in response to internal changes, such as a new business model.

The goals of business transformation are to improve performance, increase agility and adaptability, and reduce costs. To achieve these goals, organizations need to make changes at all levels, from individual employees to company-wide systems. There are different approaches to business transformation, but all share some common elements. These include identifying the need for change, developing a plan for change, implementing the plan, and monitoring and modifying the plan as needed.

Business transformation can be a complex and daunting task, but it is essential for organizations that want to stay competitive in today's ever-changing business landscape. With the right plan and execution, business transformation can help organizations achieve their goals and create a more efficient and effective organization (Müller, & Pfleger, 2014).

2.14.1. Business Model Canvas

The canvas helps businesses to create a flexible and adaptable plan that can be easily changed as the business evolves. The canvas consists of nine sections: value proposition, customer segments, channels, customer relationships, revenue streams, key resources, key activities, key partners and cost structure. Template for Business Model Canvas is shown in the below figure.

Figure 2. 10 Business Model Canvas

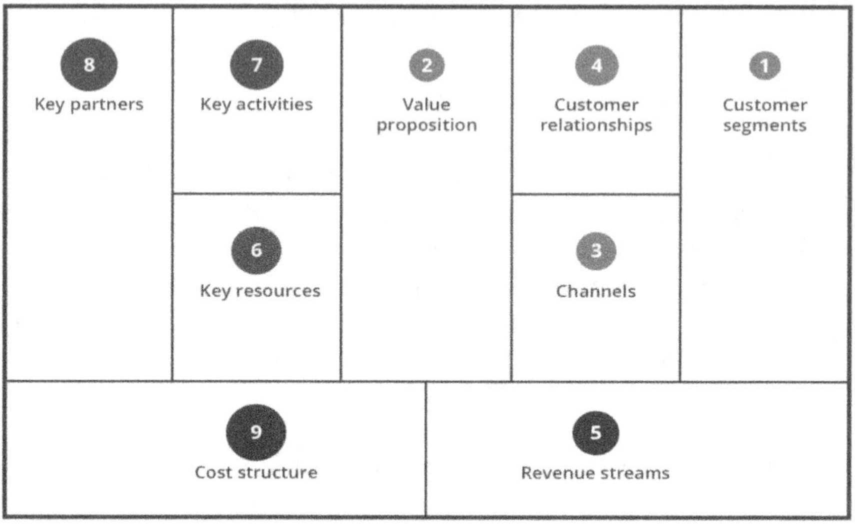

Source: Ebinum (2019)

Each section contains a number of specific questions that need to be answered in order to create a comprehensive business plan. The questions help businesses to understand their customers, their markets and their own capabilities. It is especially useful for businesses that are constantly evolving and changing. The canvas helps businesses to identify their core values and to create a plan that is responsive to the ever-changing needs of the business (Joyce & Paquin, 2016).

2.14.2. Benefits of Business Transformation

There are many benefits of business transformation, including:

➢ **Improved performance:** Business transformation can help organizations improve their performance by streamlining processes and increasing efficiency.

➢ **Increased agility and adaptability:** By making changes at all levels, businesses can become more Agile and adaptable, which is essential in today's rapidly changing world.

➢ **Reduced costs:** One of the main goals of business transformation is to reduce costs. By streamlining processes and eliminating waste, businesses can save money.

➢ **Improved employee satisfaction:** Business transformation can also lead to improved employee satisfaction by creating a more efficient and effective workplace.

➢ **Improved customer satisfaction:** By improving performance and reducing costs, businesses can also improve customer satisfaction.Challenges of Business Transformation

Business transformation can be a complex and daunting task, but it is essential for organizations that want to stay competitive in today's ever-changing business landscape. There are many challenges that organizations face when undertaking business transformation, including:

➢ **Resistance to change:** One of the biggest challenges of business transformation is overcoming resistance to change. Employees may be resistant to new processes or technologies, and it can be difficult to get them on board with the changes.

➢ **Implementation difficulties:** Another challenge is implementing the changes successfully. Business transformation can be complex, and there may be difficulties along the way.

➢ **Costs:** Business transformation can be costly, and organizations need to be prepared for the financial investment.

➢ **Time:** Business transformation can take time, and it may be several years before the full benefits are realized.

Despite the challenges, business transformation is essential for organizations that want to stay competitive in today's ever-changing business landscape. By identifying the need for change, developing a plan, and implementing the changes, businesses can overcome the challenges and reap the benefits of business transformation (Marchand & Wade, 2014).

2.14.3. Common Mistakes made during Business Transformation

According to Ruiz (2018), there are many mistakes that businesses make when undertaking business transformation, but some of the most common include:

- **Not Identifying the need for change:** One of the first mistakes businesses make is not identifying the need for change. This can lead to a lack of buy-in from employees and difficulty implementing the changes.
- **Not developing a plan:** Another mistake is not developing a comprehensive plan for business transformation. Without a plan, it can be difficult to implement the changes and track progress.
- **Implementation difficulties:** As mentioned above, implementation difficulties are one of the biggest challenges of business transformation. If businesses are not prepared for the complexity of the process, they may run into problems along the way.
- **Not monitoring progress:** Finally, businesses may fail to monitor progress during business transformation. This can lead to stagnation and a lack of results. To avoid this, businesses should establish metrics and KPIs to track progress and ensure that the transformation is on track.

With the right planning and execution, it can be a great way to improve your business transformation. The different stages in business transformation include:

1. **Define the goals**: The first step to successful business transformation is to define your goals. What do you want to achieve with your transformation? What are your key areas of focus? Once you have answers to these questions, you can begin to plan your transformation.
2. **Create a roadmap:** Once you know what your goals are, you need to create a roadmap. This will help you map out the steps you need to take to reach your goals. It should include milestones and deadlines so that you can track your progress.
3. **Assemble a team:** You cannot undertake a business transformation alone. You will need a team of experts to help

you with different aspects of the transformation. Assemble a team of people who have the skills and knowledge necessary to help you succeed.

4. **Implement changes:** Now it is time to implement the changes you have been planning. This is where the rubber meets the road. Be sure to communicate your plans to all stakeholders and get buy-in from everyone involved. Make sure you have a solid plan in place before making any changes.
5. **Evaluate your progress:** Once you have made the changes, it is time to evaluate your progress. Regular evaluation will help you course-correct and ensure that your transformation is successful.

By following the above points, companies can avoid the common mistakes during the business transformation process.

2.15. Agility in Business Transformation

In recent years, Agile has been gaining popularity as a project management approach for business transformation initiatives. There are many benefits of using Agile methodology for business transformation. One of the most important benefits is that it helps organizations to focus on value delivery and customer satisfaction. Agile methodology also helps organizations to respond quickly to changes, which is critical in today's rapidly changing business environment.

Another benefit of Agile methodology is that it promotes collaboration and teamwork among all stakeholders. This is important because business transformation projects usually involve multiple departments and/or functions. By promoting collaboration, Agile methodology enables all stakeholders to work together towards the common goal of successful business transformation.

Lastly, Agile methodology also helps organizations to manage risks better. This is because Agile projects are typically divided into small phases or sprints. This makes it easier to identify and address risks early on in the project.

Overall, Agile methodology can be a very effective tool for business transformation. It helps organizations to focus on value delivery, respond quickly to changes, and promote collaboration among all stakeholders. Additionally, Agile methodology can help organizations to better manage risks associated with business transformation initiatives (Fuchs & Hess, 2018).

2.16. Agile HR

Agile HR is a human resources management methodology that emphasizes agility, flexibility, and collaboration in order to respond quickly to changes in the business environment. It aims to create an environment where employees are able to be more productive and happier in their work. Agile HR focuses on creating a work culture that is adaptable and responsive to change, which can be beneficial for businesses that are constantly evolving. Agile HR strategies are a set of policies and/or practices for managing human resources in businesses. These policies and/or practices can offer Agile workers, for example, a collaborative workplace culture, learning organizations, design-focused work teams, and practices that empower employees (Junita, 2021).

Some of the key principles of Agile HR include:

1. valuing individuals and interactions over processes and tools;
2. focusing on customer needs and delivering value to them rapidly;
3. embracing change and being open to new ideas;
4. working in short cycles or "sprints" in order to achieve quick feedback and continuous improvement;
5. and using data to drive decision-making.

Agile HR can be applied to a wide range of human resources functions, such as recruitment, performance management, employee development, and compensation. It can also be used to help businesses create a more Agile workforce by upskilling employees and giving them the ability to work flexibly. When implemented correctly, Agile HR can help businesses to improve their performance, better respond to change, and create a more engaged and productive workforce. By structuring the HR department into interdisciplinary, empowered teams that continuously align with evolving business demands by sensing and responding through open communication while functioning in short cycles, Agile HR attempts to minimize waste and optimize the flow of value to its customers. All facets of the HR operation, including the structures, roles, procedures, and tools as well as the knowledge and conduct of HR management and HR staff, are influenced by Agile principles (McMackin & Heffernan, 2021).

2.17. Agile Marketing

Agile marketing is a type of marketing that is based on the principles of Agile software development. It is a relatively new approach to marketing that is still being refined, but it has already been shown to be very effective. Agile marketing is designed to be flexible and responsive to changes in the market, and it allows businesses to adapt quickly to new opportunities and threats. Agile marketing promotes interdepartmental cooperation, common objectives, and empowered teams. To achieve goals, learning must happen quickly (Gera & Mishra, 2019).

Agile marketing is based on the same principles as Agile software development, which are: Iterative and incremental approach; Focus on customer needs and feedback; Adaptability and flexibility and Cross-functional team collaboration. These principles are applied to the marketing process in order to make it more Agile. The iterative and incremental approach means that marketing activities are undertaken in small steps, with each step building on the previous one. This allows businesses to make changes quickly if they need to, and to test new ideas before implementing them fully. The focus on customer needs and feedback means that marketers constantly gather data about their target market and use this information to guide their decisions. This helps businesses to be more responsive to the customers (Gera & Mishra, 2019).

One of the most important marketing tenets nowadays is agility. Marketers must step up as the economy changes rapidly, more people work from home, and more companies only conduct business online. The practice of marketing is changing due to the digital transformation of businesses, the advent of new channels (such as social media and mobile devices), and a flood of client data. To put it simply, executives must focus their people, processes, and technology on the consumer and foster innovation in order to effectively implement the mandate for marketing agility (Lewnes, 2021).

2.18. Agile Project Management

Agile Project Management (APM) is a brand-new and distinctive approach to managing projects. It is already being predicted by some experts to replace traditional project management in the twenty-first century. APM has not, however, had the expected impact on project management till date. It mostly focused on IT projects (Bergmann & Karwowski, 2018).

Agile project management is a way to run projects that puts a lot of emphasis on being flexible and working together. It relies on short, iterative cycles of planning, development, and review to ensure that projects are constantly moving forward and that feedback is integrated into the next cycle. This approach is often used for software development projects, but can be applied to any type of project. Although several Agile Development techniques deal with the people, process, and technology management aspects of software projects, their main emphasis is on coding, testing, and artefact delivery. It makes sense for software development to advance by incorporating the idea of agility into project management (Alleman, 2005).

Agile project management has many benefits. It helps to reduce risk by ensuring that projects are constantly making progress and that feedback is being integrated into the next cycle. This approach also allows for more flexible responses to change, which can be essential in today's fast-paced business environment. Additionally, Agile project management can help to improve communication and collaboration among team members.

In order to practice APM, first, it is important to select the right methodology for your specific project. There are many different Agile frameworks, so it is important to choose one that will fit the needs of your team and your project. Second, you will need to have a clear understanding of the roles and responsibilities of each team member. And finally, you will need to create a robust system for tracking progress and ensuring that everyone is on the same page.

2.19. Agile Program Management

Agile Program Management is a way to manage projects that use the Agile methodology. It aids in making sure that projects are finished on schedule, within budget, and to the highest standards possible. Agile program management aids in ensuring that all stakeholders are continuously informed of project developments and that any changes or problems are dealt with as soon as they occur. Program management approaches are being adopted by organizations as a temporary step toward achieving corporate agility. This coexistence of Agile and non-Agile tasks within a program, result in new coordination difficulties. Programs that use Agile methods extensively encounter comparable difficulties collaborating with the rest of the organization, which uses non-Agile approaches (Khan, Fernandez, & Jiang, 2016).

2.20. Agile Portfolio Management

Many firms are implementing Agile service delivery teams that have a high degree of autonomy and self-organization. A matching IT portfolio management as a linking mechanism is thought to be important to promote team alignment to the enterprise strategic direction while protecting their autonomy (Horlach, Schirmer & Drews, 2019).

Agile Portfolio Management is a way of managing a portfolio of projects using Agile methods. It involves creating a prioritized list of projects, then dividing them up into smaller batches and working on them one at a time. This helps to ensure that the most important projects are given priority and that the portfolio is always moving forward.

Agile Portfolio Management can be used for both large and small portfolios. For large portfolios, it can help to keep track of progress and ensure that projects are completed in a timely manner. For smaller portfolios, it can help to ensure that all projects are given the attention they deserve and that nothing falls through the cracks.

There are many benefits to using Agile Portfolio Management. It helps to ensure that projects are given the attention they need, and that they are completed in a timely manner. It also helps to avoid scope creep, which can often occur when working on larger projects. In addition, Agile methods can help to improve communication between project members and stakeholders, as well as provide better visibility into the project's progress.

The most important thing to remember when using Agile Portfolio Management is that it will not solve all of your problems, but it can help to make your project more successful. Organizations should learn about portfolio management, its connections to other governance processes including investment decisions, architecture, and sourcing management, as well as how these processes relate to agility. Companies are urged to investigate how to incorporate support activities like HR, accounting, or legal in this arrangement as a result of extending agility outside of software development (Horlach, Schirmer & Drews, 2019).

2.21. PRINCE2 Agile – The Agile Project Management

According to Prince2 (n.d.), PRINCE2 (PRojects IN Controlled Environments) is a process-based method for effective project management. (Prince2, n.d.) The most comprehensive Agile project management system available today, PRINCE2 Agile combines the responsiveness and adaptability of Agile with the structured framework of PRINCE2.

In order for the approach to be utilized in conjunction with Agile behaviors, concepts, frameworks, and techniques, PRINCE2 Agile explains how to setup and tune PRINCE2. Agile can be used for both projects and normal ongoing work, but PRINCE2 and PRINCE2 Agile are only appropriate for usage on projects ("PRINCE2 Agile in 1000 Words," 2021).

Figure 2. 11 PRINCE2 Agile, combined with PRINCE2 with Agile working practices

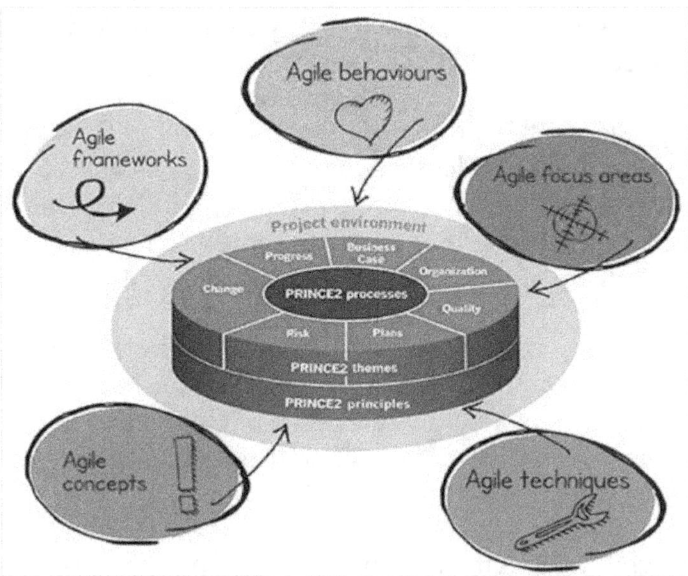

Source: Adopted from "PRINCE2 Agile in 1000 Words," 2021

The above picture describes about using Agile project management best practices when that is the delivery method of choice. It is not necessary to modify Agile to comply with

PRINCE2. Agile and PRINCE2 each have their own advantages. Together, they strengthen one another to produce a comprehensive strategy for Agile project management. We can realize the potential of both if we approach this combination as a blend. The customization of PRINCE2 is driven by a true awareness and comprehension of Agile thinking.

The most comprehensive Agile project management system available today, PRINCE2 Agile combines the responsiveness and adaptability of Agile with the structured framework of PRINCE2. PRINCE2 Agile offers suggestions on how PRINCE2 can:

- establish a productive environment for an Agile project;
- encourage and promote Agile delivery
- finish a project when Agile deems it necessary to do so.

All of these points are connected by a thorough and sincere analysis of Agile approaches and their worth in producing effective project outcomes ("PRINCE2 Agile in 1000 Words," 2021).

Whatever the project delivery method, PRINCE2 Agile resets expectations and demonstrates PRINCE2's capacity to do so. In addition to showing how well PRINCE2 and Agile will work together, PRINCE2 Agile is the ideal "how to" manual for modern project management.

The two most popular Agile frameworks, Scrum and Kanban, are covered in PRINCE2 Agile. The backdrop for the frameworks is provided by the Scrum Guide and the Kanban Method, and how they might operate together is explained by PRINCE2 Agile.

PRINCE2 Agile is a hybrid solution that combines the strengths of both methodologies (PRINCE2 and Agile) and generates additional value.

PRINCE2

- Trustworthy governance.

- Best practises for project management and project working that have been shown.
- A linguistic and terminology standard that is applied internationally.
- A technique that can be customised to your unique business, project, and strategy.
- Encourages lessons learned and ongoing development.

Agile way of working

- Early and frequent customer value delivery.
- Incremental and iterative solutions that involve stakeholders.
- The ability to adapt and think strategically in uncertain times.
- Frameworks that support retrospectives and a philosophy of learning as you go.
- Actions that promote empowered and cooperative working methods.

Together, these two components of the solution create an environment where self-managed techniques can engage stakeholders and faithfully record the details while implementing governance processes to guarantee that projects are well managed and in line with business plans and programs. PRINCE2 Agile is designed for success. It is a clever and smart solution that combines the top principles and ideas for project management and delivery (PRINCE2 Agile in 1000 Words, 2021).

2.22. Agile Approaches/Methodologies/Frameworks

Agile is not a methodology or framework. Agile is principally about mindset, more attitude than process, more environment than methodology, more than a movement – it is business imperative. Agile is set of 4 values and 12 principles (discussed in section 2.1.2). Agile can be seen as umbrella term, under several methodologies exist (Abbas, Gravell & Wills, 2008).

Figure 2. 12 Agile Umbrella

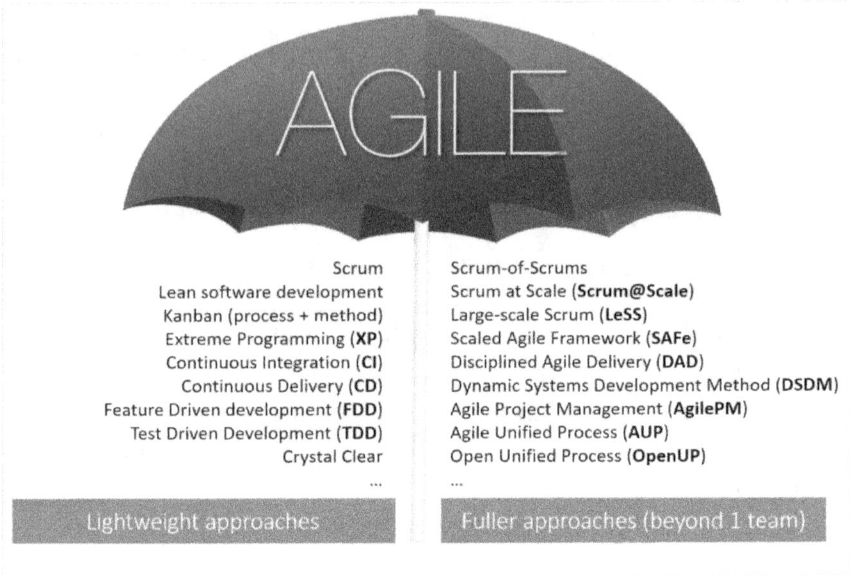

Source: https://teamhood.com/

As seen in the above figure, there are several methodologies under the Agile umbrella, they all share some common principles as below:

- **Iterative and Incremental Development:** All Agile approaches are iterative, which means that they involve repeating cycles of work (called iterations) until the project is complete. They are also incremental, which means that new functionality is delivered in each iteration.
- **Working Software:** The goal of Agile approaches is to deliver working software frequently, typically every two weeks or less. This gives stakeholders the ability to see progress and give feedback early and often.
- **Self-Organizing Teams:** Agile approaches rely on self-organizing teams, which means that teams are empowered to make decisions about how they work. This is in contrast to traditional approaches where management makes all the decisions.
- **Face-to-Face Communication:** Agile approaches emphasize face-to-face communication over other forms of

communication (such as email or instant messaging). This helps ensure that everyone is on the same page and reduces the need for documentation.

- **Customer Involvement:** Agile approaches involve customers in the development process so that they can provide feedback early and often. This helps ensure that the final product meets their needs.

Agile methodologies are two-fold, one is light weight approaches and the second is fuller approaches. In the following sections these approaches are elaborated.

2.22.1. Light Weight Approaches

Below is the overview of Lightweight Agile frameworks.

2.22.1.1. Scrum

Scrum is a framework for managing software development projects. It is an iterative and incremental approach that helps teams deliver valuable software products in a timely and predictable manner. Product owners work with development teams to identify and prioritize the work that needs to be done. This is typically done in the form of user stories, which are short descriptions of the functionality that users need.

Scrum is a very popular Agile approach that has been around for a long time. It is based on the idea of self-organizing teams who work in short sprints to deliver working software incrementally. The systems development process is described by SCRUM as a loose collection of activities that mixes tried-and-true methods with the greatest solutions a development team can come up with for creating systems. Controls are employed to manage the process and inherent risk because these activities are loose. The popular iterative/incremental object-oriented development cycle has been improved with SCRUM (Schwaber, 1997).

Figure 2. 13 Scrum Process

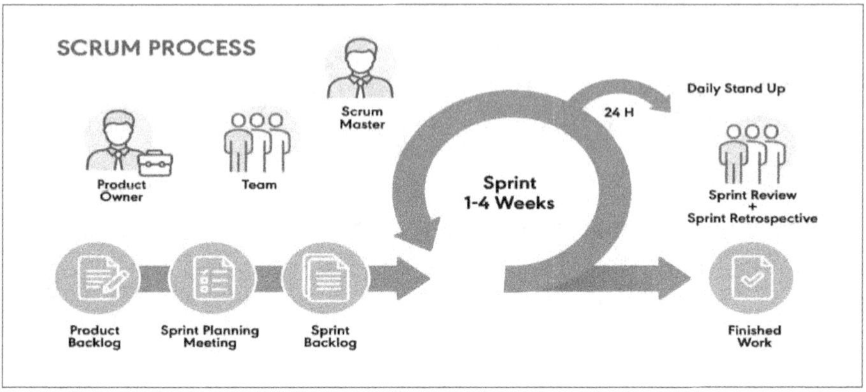

Source: www.pm-partners.com.au

Development teams use sprints, or time-boxed periods, to complete the work. Each sprint begins with a planning meeting, where the product owner and development team discuss the user stories that need to be completed. The team then commits to completing a certain amount of work within the sprint.

During the sprint, the team holds daily stand-up meetings to inspect progress and identify any impediments. At the end of the sprint, the team demo their work to the product owner and stakeholders. The scrum framework is designed to help teams deliver valuable software products in a timely and predictable manner. It is an iterative and incremental approach that enables development teams to adapt to changing requirements. Scrum is a popular Agile framework that is used by many organizations.

2.22.1.2. Lean Software Development

Lean Software Development is a software development methodology that seeks to minimize waste and maximize value. It is based on the principle that if you cannot measure it, you cannot improve it. Lean software development is particularly well-suited for projects with unpredictable deadlines and changing requirements. It focuses on delivering working software as quickly as possible, and then continually improving the product based on feedback from users.

Figure 2. 14 Lean Software Development

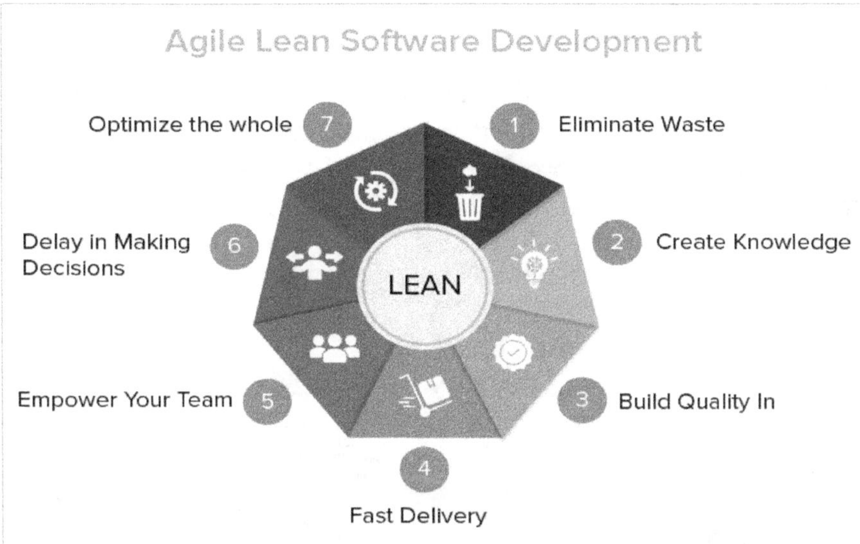

Source: www://appinventiv.com/

Some of the key principles of lean software development are as follows:

1. Eliminate waste.
2. Deliver value to the customer quickly.
3. Focus on the user's needs.
4. Continuously improve the process.

Minimizing work in progress is a crucial lean principle that forces any production issues into the open right away. Then, production is stopped so that each issue with the system creating the goods may be resolved once and for all. Although initially irritating, the outcome is very high levels of production and quality (Middleton, 2001).

2.22.1.3. Kanban

Kanban is another popular Agile framework that emphasizes continuous delivery and process improvement. The key advantages of applying the Kanban technique include shorter lead times for software delivery, better software quality, better collaboration and communication, more regular delivery, and fewer problems that customers report. The difficulties include diverse organizational problems, a lack of expertise and specialized training, and others (Ahmad, Markkula & Oivo, 2013).

The key principles of Kanban are as follows:

1. Visualize the work flow.
2. Limit work in progress (WIP).
3. Focus on continuous delivery.
4. Improve collaboratively, evolve experimentally.

Figure 2. 15 Kanban Board

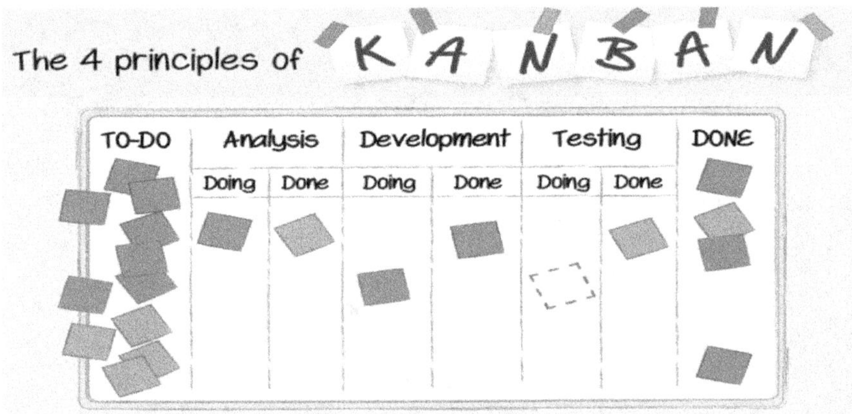

Source: www.knowledgetrain.co.uk

With Kanban, teams can visualize the work flow and limit WIP for each stage of the process. This helps to identify bottlenecks and optimize the process. In addition, Kanban focuses on continuous delivery, which means that new features or products are delivered frequently. Finally, Kanban teams improve collaboratively and evolve experimentally. This allows them to constantly improve their process and adapt to change.

2.22.1.4. ScrumBan

ScrumBan is a modified version of the Scrum software development methodology that incorporates aspects of the Kanban methodology. It is designed to be more flexible than traditional Scrum, and can be used for projects of any size. ScrumBan can be adapted to fit the needs of any organization, and is often used in cases where traditional Scrum has been found to be too inflexible. It is also well-suited for projects that are constantly changing or evolving, as it allows for more flexibility in terms of how work is completed. ScrumBan has many of the same principles as Scrum, including the use of sprints, user stories, and backlogs. However, it also incorporates aspects of Kanban, such as the use of a kanban board to visualize work progress. This helps to make the ScrumBan process more transparent and easier to understand for all team members.

Scrumban is a management paradigm for enhancing software engineering techniques that combines the strengths of Scrum and Kanban. Scrumban is anticipated to replace both Scrum and Kanban because it incorporates their best elements. Scrumban might have a favorable impact on problems like the consistency of many sites, communication, and cultural concerns, as well as resource sharing between sites (Banijamali, et al, 2016).

2.22.1.5. Extreme Programming (XP)

eXtreme Programming (XP) is a more controversial Agile approach that has been around since the early days of Agile. It is based on the idea of delivering working software frequently, using short iterations and constant feedback from customers.

XP is a software development methodology which emphasizes teamwork, communication, and customer satisfaction. It is designed to be adaptable to the individual project and team, and aims to produce high-quality software quickly and efficiently. Extreme programming (XP), a quick application development methodology, is one example of an Agile applications development technique that focuses on refining technical implementation and feature requirements (Sohaib, Osama, et al, 2019).

XP is based on the following values:

- **Communication:** All members of the team should be involved in every decision, and communication should be open and honest.
- **Feedback:** Feedback from customers and other stakeholders should be used to improve the software.
- **Simplicity:** The software should be as simple as possible, and unnecessary features should be avoided.
- **Courage:** The team should be brave enough to make changes when necessary, even if it means going back to square one.
- **Respect:** Everyone on the team should respect each other and their opinions.

IT Companies should focus on the above values to produce high-quality software quickly and efficiently.

2.22.1.6. Continuous Integration (CI)

Continuous Integration (CI) is a way of making software in which developers merge their code changes several times a day into a shared repository. Each merge is then verified by an automated build to ensure that the new code does not break the existing application. If the build is successful, the code changes are automatically deployed to a testing or staging environment. This practice enables developers to get feedback on their code changes very quickly and helps to avoid the "integration hell" (Mohammad, 2017) that can happen when code changes from different developers' conflict with each other. There are a number of popular CI tools available, such as Jenkins, Travis CI and CircleCI (Mohammad, 2017).

2.22.1.7. Continuous Delivery (CD)

Continuous Delivery (CD) is a software engineering practice where code is checked in and out of a source control repository frequently during development. This allows the team to detect errors early and fix them promptly. When the code is ready, it is deployed to a testing environment for further validation. If all goes well, the code is then deployed to a production environment. CD involves automating the build, test, and deployment process. This allows for rapid feedback and constant progress tracking. CD is often used in conjunction with Agile methodology, which focuses on delivering software incrementally and frequently.

The main benefits of CD are:

- **Reduced risk:** By reducing the time between code changes and deployments, CD minimizes the risk of errors.
- **Faster feedback:** CD provides faster feedback loops, which helps developers identify and fix errors quickly.
- **Increased collaboration:** CD encourages collaboration between developers, testers, and operations team members.
- **Improved quality:** Automating the build and deployment process ensures that only high-quality code is released to production.

CD is a key enabler of DevOps, which is a set of practices that aim to improve the collaboration between development and operations teams (Mohammad, 2017).

2.22.1.8. Feature Driven Development (FDD)

Feature Driven Development (FDD) is a software development approach that stresses the importance of features and their interactions, rather than on comprehensive design documents. In FDD, features are identified, designed, and tested in an iterative and incremental manner. FDD is an Agile method for making software that can be used with other Agile methods like XP or Scrum (Budoya, C., Kissaka, M., & Mtebe, J. 2019).

The key practices of FDD are:

1. Develop an overall model. This includes identifying the major components of the system and how they interact.
2. Build a features list. This is a prioritized list of the functionality that needs to be implemented.
3. Plan by feature. For each feature on the list, create a plan that includes who will do the work, what tasks need to be completed, and when the feature will be delivered.
4. Design by feature. Create detailed designs for each feature on the list. These designs should be reviewed and approved by stakeholders before implementation.
5. Build by feature. Implement the features on the list one at a time. Each feature should be thoroughly tested before moving on to the next one.
6. Integration and Testing: FDD integrates features as they are completed, rather than waiting until all features are finished. This allows for early feedback and reduces the risk of integration problems later on.
7. Releasing: When all the features on the list have been implemented, the system is ready for release.

The above features of FDD help ther companies to produce quality software quickly and efficiently.

2.22.1.9. Test Driven Development (TDD)

Test-driven development (TDD) is a way of making software that uses a very short development cycle over and over again: red, green, refactor. The process is based on the belief that if you cannot write a good test case, you do not understand the code well enough to write good code. TDD has been around for a while, but it is only recently that it is gained popularity in the Agile community. TDD is often used in conjunction with Extreme Programming (XP), which is another Agile software development methodology (George & Williams, 2004).

There are three main benefits to using TDD:

1. It helps you write better code
2. It forces you to think about edge cases and potential errors

3. It makes it easier to refactor code later on

The above benefits of using TDD makes it convenient for the companies to adopt it in the development of products.

2.22.1.10. Crystal Clear

Crystal Clear is a lightweight Agile framework that helps teams work smarter by focusing on the most important things. It was created by Jeff Patton and is based on the principles of Agile software development. Crystal Clear is meant to be used on small to medium-sized projects where the team needs to be able to move quickly and adjust to change.

Crystal Clear is based on four key concepts: communication, collaboration, feedback, and adaptation. These concepts are embodied in the framework's seven core values: customer satisfaction, teamwork, continuous improvement, simplicity, self-organization, courage, and respect. Crystal Clear is a flexible framework that can be tailored to the needs of any project. It is also easy to learn and use, making it a good choice for teams who are new to Agile software development (Chang, 2010).

2.22.2. Fuller Approaches

2.22.2.1. Scrum-of Scrums

As shown in the below figure, the Scrum-of-Scrums is a framework for managing multiple scrums. It allows for the coordination of work between different scrum teams by having a representative from each team attend a meeting where they can report on their progress and share any blockers. This framework helps ensure that all teams are working towards the same goal and that dependencies are managed effectively (Qurashi & Qureshi, 2014).

Figure 2. 16 Scrum of Scrums

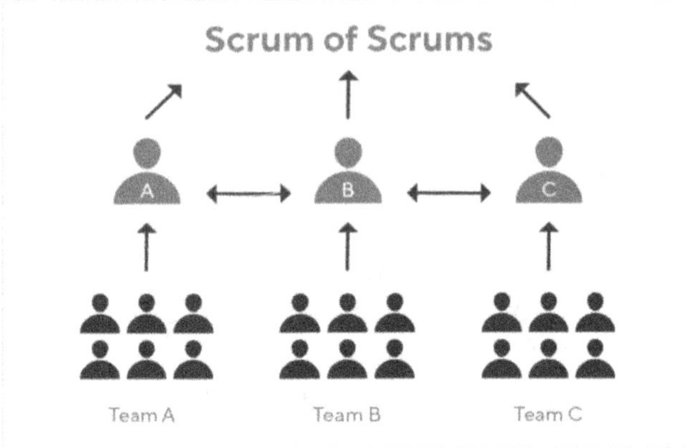

Source: www.wrike.com

2.22.2.2. Scrum at Scale (Scrum@Scale)

There are a few different frameworks that can be used when scaling scrum. One of these frameworks is called "Scrum@Scale." This framework is designed to help organizations that are looking to scale scrum beyond a single team. It does this by providing a set of guidelines and principles that can be used to create a scalable scrum framework (Ozkan, Tarhan, & Kucuk, 2017).

Figure 2. 17 Scrum@Scale Framework

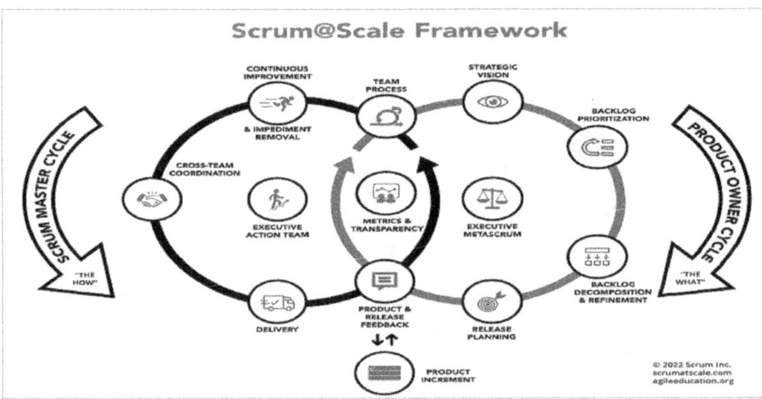

Source: www.digite.com

As shown in the above figure Scrum@Scale offers several roles and events in order to scale the scrum on enterprise level.

2.22.2.3. Solutions for Agile Governance in the Enterprise (SAGE)

SAGE is a solution for Agile governance in the enterprise. SAGE provides a framework for managing Agile projects and helps ensure that everyone is working towards the same goal. With SAGE, you will have everything you need to successfully implement Agile within your organization (Thompson, 2019). SAGE is:

- A flexible framework that can be tailored to your organization's needs
- Scalable, so it can grow with your organization
- Designed for the enterprise, so it can be used by large organizations
- Easy to use, so you will be up and running in no time

The above benefits of using SAGE make it suitable for the companies to adopt it in the development of products.

2.22.2.4. Large Scale Scrum (LeSS)

LeSS is a framework for scaling Agile practices to large numbers of people. It was created by Craig Larman and Bas Vodde, and is based on the Scrum framework. LeSS is designed to be simple to understand and easy to adopt, and can be implemented with a minimum of training and overhead (Larman, Vodde, & Jensen, 2017).

Figure 2. 18 Large Scale Scrum (LeSS)

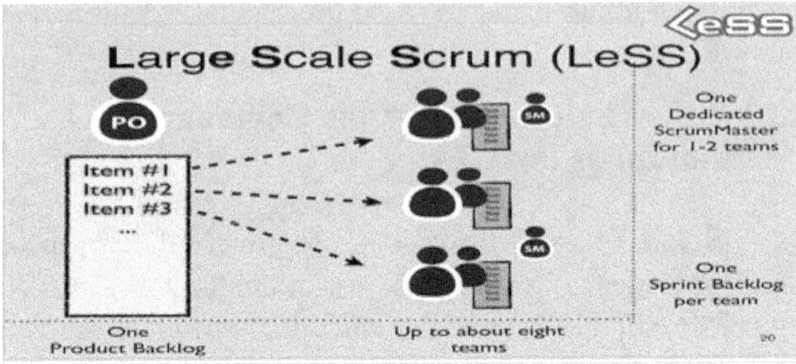

Source: www.infoq.com

Structure of the teams in LeSS can be seen in the above figure.

2.22.2.5. Scaled Agile Framework (SAFe)

Scaled Agile Framework (SAFe) is an Agile framework that allows teams to work in parallel, completing tasks as they are ready. This leads to faster turnaround times and fewer budget overruns. SAFe is a flexible framework that can be customized to fit the needs of any organization. SAFe promotes collaboration and communication between team members, which leads to better results. SAFe helps organizations to avoid the pitfalls of waterfall project management, such as missed deadlines and budget overruns (Turetken, Stojanov, & Trienekens, 2017).

Leveraging the power of Scaled Agile Framework lets companies make quicker choices, communicate more effectively, streamline operations, and stay focused on the customer. Built-in quality is one of the key SAFe values: it stresses the significance of integrating quality into every phase of the development cycle. By enabling high-performing teams and teams of teams to cut out wasteful tasks, spot and fix delays, constantly improve, and make sure they are creating the correct things, SAFe offers quantifiable increases in productivity. Knowledge workers can attain autonomy, mastery, and purpose, which are the important elements in unlocking intrinsic motivation, with the use of the Scaled Agile Framework, which is another advantage of scaling Agile.

Figure 2. 19 Scaled Agile Framework (SAFe) Big Picture

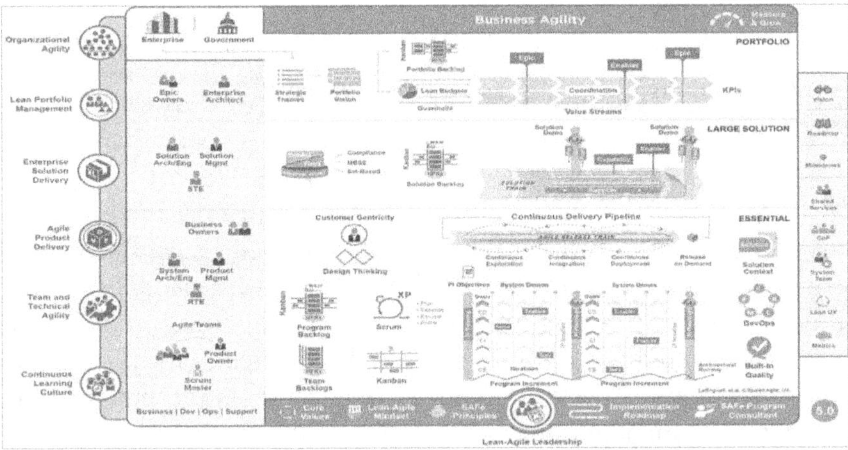

Source: https://www.scaledAgileframework.com/

2.22.2.6. Disciplined Agile Delivery (DAD)

Disciplined Agile Delivery (DAD) is an Agile framework that combines the best of Scrum and XP with Kanban-style visual management to help you deliver software in a more timely and predictable manner. With DAD, you will be able to manage your workflow better while still being able to respond quickly to changes. DAD is a great option for organizations that want to improve their software delivery process. It can help you avoid many of the common pitfalls that lead to delays and cost overruns. (Ambler & Lines, 2020)

The tool kit for Disciplined Agile (DA) offers organizations clear guidance that can assist them in streamlining their processes in a manner that is sensitive to the context. This helps build a solid foundation for business agility by showing how all the different activities, like finance, portfolio management, solution delivery (software development), IT operations, enterprise architecture, vendor management, and a lot of others, work together. DA also provides a description of what these activities should be addressing, as well as a variety of options for achieving this goal, and a description of the trade-offs associated with each option (S. Ambler & Lines, 2012).

2.22.2.7. Dynamic Systems Development Method (DSDM)

DSDM is an Agile framework that enables organizations to deliver high quality software quickly and efficiently. With DSDM, teams can respond to change while still delivering on time and within budget. DSDM is founded on eight principles: active user involvement, frequent delivery, collaborative teamwork, iterative and incremental development, requirements management, configuration management, project planning, and testing. These principles are embodied in the DSDM Agile Process Cycle, which consists of four phases: Pre-Project, Feasibility Study, Foundations, and Implementation.

Figure 2. 20 DSDM Life Cycle

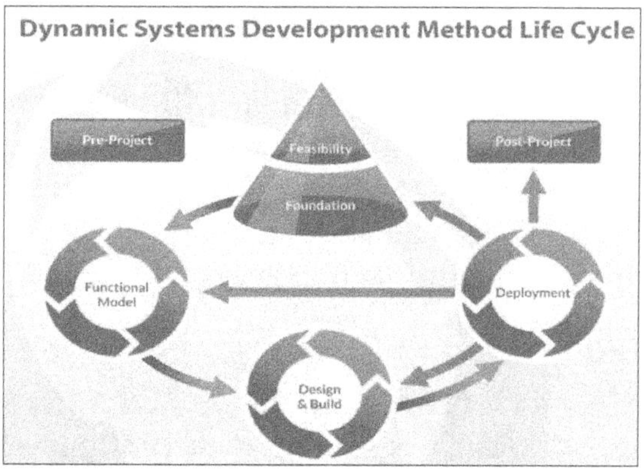

Source: Pinterest

The DSDM lifecycle is iterative and incremental, meaning that new functionality is delivered in small increments. This allows for constant feedback from users and helps to ensure that the final product meets their needs. The DSDM framework is flexible and can be adapted to fit the needs of any organization. It is well suited for projects that are large and complex, as well as those that are smaller in scope (Stapleton, 1999).

2.22.2.8. Agile Project Management (AgilePM)

AgilePM is a specific Agile framework that focuses on delivering projects in a more controlled and predictable way. It is based on the values and principles of agility, and uses a subset of the Scrum framework. AgilePM is a great choice for organizations who want to reap the benefits of agility, but need more structure and predictability than what Scrum can provide. The framework provides clear roles, responsibilities, and guidelines that make it easier to deliver successful projects (Uikey & Suman, 2012).

2.22.2.9. Agile Unified Process (AUP)

The Agile Unified Process (AUP) is a framework for Agile software development. It is based on the principles of Agile software development, and includes practices from Scrum, Extreme Programming (XP), and other Agile methods. The AUP is designed to help organizations transition from traditional, waterfall-based development processes to an Agile process. The AUP provides a framework for developers to follow during the software development process. It includes best practices for Agile software development, and helps developers transition from traditional waterfall processes to an Agile process. The AUP is based on the principles of Agile software development, and includes practices from Scrum, Extreme Programming (XP), and other Agile methods (Edeki, 2013).

2.22.2.10. Open Unified Process (OpenUP)

The Open Unified Process (OpenUP) provides a standardized, yet flexible, framework for Agile software development that can be tailored to the specific needs of your organization. This process has been proven to improve communication and collaboration between team members, while also accelerating project delivery.

OpenUP is an Agile framework that can be customized to fit the specific needs of your organization. It is based on four core values: communication, collaboration, customer focus, and delivery. By following the OpenUP framework, you can improve communication and collaboration between team members, while also accelerating project delivery (Nascimento & Oliveira, 2012).

2.22.2.11. AgileSHIFT Framework

Axelos (2018) asserts that the majority of firms today aim to change the way they operate. Regardless of the industry they are retail, telecom, or public services—their established methods of operation may not be sufficient to stay competitive and survive. This transformation has been prompted by things like:

- Rising customer demands and expectations
- Increasing disruptive rivals (often taking use of new technologies),
- legacy or archaic procedures are no longer useful,
- and business cultures do not support operating in a fast-paced market.

It is imperative to transform. It is also difficult. Due to this, AgileSHIFT was established, a new method of working that aims to foster an enterprise agility culture while assisting in preparing people and organizations for transformative shift. AgileSHIFT was created to make it possible for people, teams, and organizations to thrive in a VUCA environment. This culture shift is fueled by understanding and distilling the mindset behind Agile ways of working and exploiting them throughout the entire organization, not just by adopting an Agile approach or tool.

AgileSHIFT does this by:

- showing how an enterprise agility culture is advantageous to organizations undergoing transformation and highlighting common hurdles to success;
- motivating the entire organization to accept and embrace the need for change and transformation.
- A straightforward Agile framework is provided for companies and teams to adopt
- implement, along with an overview of popular Agile ways of working and how they connect to corporate agility.

Five principles and five practices for the entire organization make up the framework along with a delivery approach that iteratively incorporates roles, skills, workflow, tools, and methodologies. Together, these factors make it possible for the entire organization to adopt agility. These elements are visually summarized in the figure below (Axelos, 2018).

Figure 2. 21 The why, what and how elements of the AgileSHIFT framework

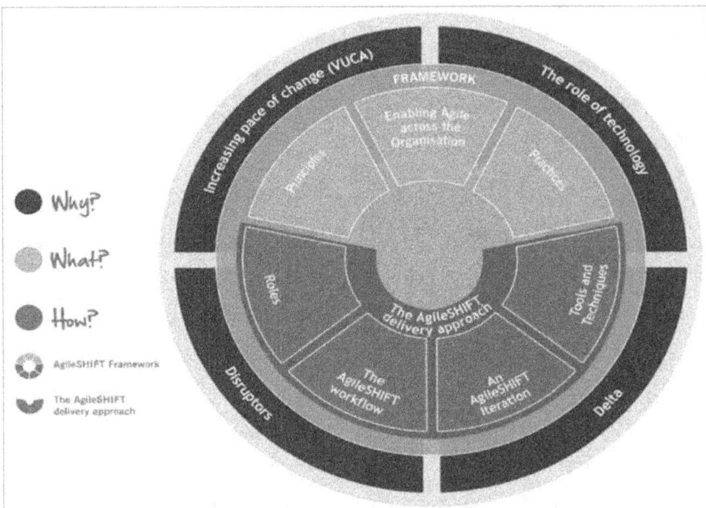

Source: A Guide to AgileSHIFT, Axelos (2018)

After analyzing "why" we require AgileSHIFT, we must now concentrate on "what" and "how," as seen in the above image.

The following components make up the AgileSHIFT framework:

- An enabler of Agile ways of working: How strategic alignment throughout the entire company is essential for effective transformation.
- AgileSHIFT guiding principles: a set of essential concepts that serve as a company's road map under all conditions.
- AgileSHIFT practises: A collection of doable strategies that will help any team that wants to work more nimbly.

These elements embrace the agility.

The AgileSHIFT way of delivering: This method covers

- **Three Important roles:** the AgileSHIFT team, the AgileSHIFT coach, and the AgileSHIFT sponsor, as well as how a team can work better.
- **The Workflow of AgileSHIFT:** A series of steps that repeat, where the team works for short amounts of time and then gets feedback and makes a decision.
- **An iteration of AgileSHIFT:** In-depth look at the things that happen during an iteration.
- **Tools and techniques:** These can be used in any AgileSHIFT project where they will be most helpful.

The delivery strategy called AgileSHIFT: This strategy takes into account

- How a team may work more efficiently as well as three crucial roles: the AgileSHIFT team, the AgileSHIFT coach, and the AgileSHIFT sponsor.
- The workflow for AgileSHIFT: a series of iterative processes where the team works in spurts, gets input, and then makes a conclusion.
- An iteration of AgileSHIFT a thorough examination of an iteration's activities.
- Resources and methods You can use these as necessary to support any AgileSHIFT endeavour. (Axelos, 2018)

These functions, processes, and iterations will aid in giving the Agile style of working structure.

2.23. Overcoming Cultural Barriers with Agile

In today's globalized economy, it is more important than ever for businesses to be able to work effectively with teams from around the world. However, cultural differences can often create communication barriers that impede productivity and efficiency. Agile practices can help overcome these cross-cultural barriers by promoting transparency and collaboration among team members. In the present study, we will explore how Agile practices can help your business overcome cross-cultural barriers and achieve success in a global marketplace.

When it comes to cultural differences in the workplace, there can be many potential sources of conflict. In the context of an IT project, one of the most common sources of conflict is when team members are working in different time zones. This can create problems when team members need to collaborate or when there is a need for real-time communication.

Another source of conflict can arise when team members from different cultures have different expectations about how work should be done. For example, some cultures may place a high value on individual contribution, while others may emphasize collective responsibility. This can lead to clashes over who is responsible for what, and how tasks should be prioritized.

In order to overcome these cultural barriers, it is important for teams to establish clear expectations and protocols for communication. The use of Agile development practices can be helpful in this regard, as it encourages close collaboration and regular communication among team members. By using Agile practices, teams can create a more cohesive and productive working environment, even in the face of cultural differences.

One major barrier to agility in distributed teams with members from a hierarchical culture is the inflexible structure of these cultures. Hierarchical cultures are often driven by tradition and a need for control, which can make it difficult to change direction or make decisions quickly. In addition, members of hierarchical cultures may be less likely to challenge authority or offer new ideas, which can limit creativity and collaboration. Additionally, these cultural norms can lead to conflict and communication problems in virtual teams.

When developing software in a distributed environment, it is important to take cultural differences into account. Culture can impact the way people communicate, Problem solving, and working. When working with distributed Agile teams, it is important to be aware of these cultural differences and to use Agile practices that can help overcome any cross-cultural barriers. Some of the most important Agile practices when working in a distributed environment include:

- **Regular communication:** In a distributed environment, it is often difficult to stay in touch with team members who are located in other parts of the world. Regular communication is essential for ensuring that everyone is on the same page and for avoiding any misunderstandings. This can be done through regular team meetings, updates, and/or status reports.
- **Frequent delivery of working software:** In a distributed environment, it can be difficult to get everyone on the same page in terms of what needs to be done and when it needs to be done. By delivering working software frequently, you can ensure that everyone is constantly updated on what has been completed and what still needs to be done. This also helps avoid any misunderstandings about the project status or goals.
- **Regular reflection:** In a distributed environment, it is easy for team members to become isolated from one another. It is therefore important to take time for regular reflection so that everyone can share their thoughts and ideas about the project and about how they are working together. This can help identify any potential problems early on and prevent them from becoming bigger issues down the road.
- **Open and honest communication:** In a distributed environment, it is often difficult to read body language or understand tone. This can lead to miscommunication and misunderstandings. To avoid this, it is important to have open and

honest communication with team members. This means being clear and concise when communicating, as well as being willing to listen to others' perspectives.

When working in a distributed environment, it is important to be aware of the potential cross-cultural barriers that could impact the project. By using Agile practices such as regular communication, frequent delivery of working software, regular reflection, and open and honest communication, you can help overcome these barriers and ensure successful project delivery. When working with teams from different cultures, it is important to promote transparency and collaboration. Agile practices can help to achieve this by providing a framework for team members to communicate and work together effectively.

For example, the use of daily stand-ups and sprint planning can help ensure that everyone is on the same page and aware of what needs to be done. In addition, the use of Agile practices can help to foster a sense of ownership and responsibility among team members. This is because each team member is involved in the decision-making process and has a stake in the success of the project.

When working in a distributed Agile team, it is important to be aware of the cultural differences between team members. Culture can play a major role in how people communicate and interact with one another. In order to overcome any potential cultural barriers, it is important to be flexible and adaptable, and to use Agile practices that will help to promote communication and collaboration. Some of the most effective Agile practices for working with distributed teams include daily stand-ups, retrospectives, and problem-solving workshops. These practices help to keep everyone on the same page, and allow team members to share information and collaborate effectively. By using these practices, distributed teams can overcome any cultural barriers that may exist and work together effectively to achieve their goals.

Another way that Agile practices can help overcome cross-cultural barriers is by providing a flexible approach to work. This is because Agile practices emphasize continuous improvement and allow for changes to be made quickly and easily. This flexibility can be beneficial when working with teams from different cultures, as it allows for the incorporation of new ideas and perspectives. In addition, the use of Agile practices can help to eliminate hierarchy within organizations. This is because decision-making is decentralized and everyone is treated as an equal member of the team. Overall, Agile practices can help businesses overcome cross-cultural barriers by promoting transparency, collaboration, and flexibility. By using these practices, businesses can create an environment that is conducive to success in a global marketplace (Šmite, Gonzalez-Huerta, & Moe, 2020).

CHAPTER 3

3. REVIEW OF LITERATURE

3.1. Literature Review for Research Objective#1

In this section some concepts will be discussed related to research objective#1: Identify the challenges that IT organizations face during Agile transformation.

3.1.1. Agile Transformation Challenges

Agile practitioner problems come in many different forms and are interconnected. Some difficulties, like implementing Agile in a non-Agile setting, are multifaceted, have an impact on numerous practice areas, and can manifest themselves concurrently as organizational, social, and adaption issues. While certain issues, like evaluating Agile value or comprehending cultural change, are persistent and difficult to solve, others, like adoption, shift in importance with time (Gregory, et al, 2016).

In distributed software development (DSD), a wide physic al distance, several time zones, and cultural differences cause poo r communication that has a negative impact on the project (Shrivastava, 2010).

Lack of team ownership, ambiguous management signals, inefficient cost management, and inaccurate delivery estimates were the main issues (Ma'arif, Hafifi Yusof & Mohd Satar, 2018).

The majority of Agile transformation failures are caused by external forces. These days, many businesses are bound by either fixed-outcome or fixed-price contracts. If not, they are compelled to engage with partners who are unwilling or unable to switch to an Agile Delivery Model. One of the major obstacles to Agile transformation is culture change. Dependencies must be taken into account when tackling the issues of Agile transformation. The ineffective communication between teams is one of the main obstacles to an Agile transformation (Paula, 2022).

Mersino (2018) suggests that some of the potential obstacles to agile development include reliant waterfall teams, traditional PMO groups, centralized quality groups, functional silos, bureaucracy, vendors, and audit. An organizational culture that is incompatible with agile values, a general resistance to change within the organization, a lack of top management support and sponsorship, insufficient training and education, inconsistent processes and practices across teams, a lack of availability of business, customer, or product owner, and the widespread use of traditional development techniques are the primary barriers to the adoption of agile methodologies.

The depth and breadth of an Agile transformation necessitate agreement at a high level on the aim, the value it would bring, and a workable plan for accomplishing it, even while we discourage attempts to define an end state in minute detail. In order to assure value delivery, the operating model is designed with the identified value drivers as a guide. Metrics are then developed to track value capture during deployment. Failure to do so may limit the impact of the transition (Handscomb et al., 2022).

According to the survey 'VersionOne 12th Annual State of Agile Report' conducted in 2017, surprisingly, managers and leaders are frequently the most significant barrier to Agile transformation. It is an intriguing conundrum: managers and leaders often say they want to be more Agile, but they are often the ones who get in the way of adoption or transformation of the methodology. It would be the same as me saying that I want six pack abs but that I do not want to work out or eat healthy food. What I say and what I do are two completely different things. Consequently, why do I say that managers are making Agile less effective? In the first place, it is something that I have observed taking place at one organization after another. The actions and outcomes can be under the direct or indirect control of managers and leaders. Second, surveys have demonstrated it. In the VersionOne Annual State of Agile Report, there is a question regarding the obstacles that prevent further adoption of Agile practices. Respondents continue to point the finger at leadership as the factor that slows down the adoption of Agile practices (Mersino, 2018).

Figure 3. 1 Top Barriers to Agile Adoption

TOP BARRIERS TO AGILE ADOPTION

	2010	2017
Organizational culture at odds with agile values	51%	53%
General organization resistance to change	40%	46%
Inadequate management support and sponsorship	34%	42%
Lack of skills/experience with agile methods	40%	41%
Insufficient training and education		35%
Inconsistent processes and practices across teams		34%
Lack of business/customer/product owner availability	29%	31%
Pervasiveness of traditional development methods		30%

Source: VersionOne 12th Annual State of Agile Report

The responses received for the 12th Annual Report, which was completed in 2017, are compared to the responses obtained in 2010 in the graph that is located above. It is extremely interesting to think about the "barriers" that different organizations have identified and how they all relate to leadership. It is also important to point out that the results have not changed significantly over the course of the past five years. The obstacles faced by managers are, if anything, more difficult to overcome than they were in the past (Mersino, 2018).

As stated in above survey results, leadership is one of the barrier/challenges for successful Agile transformation. Leaders should "Trust but confirm" as stated by Ambler & Lines (2012), Leadership should have faith in their members to make right things. However, leadership must use metrics to track what is happening, which identifies the teams that may require help and support.

Leadership should ask these questions themselves to identify the needed metrics.

- Are these teams providing the quality we have come to expect?
- Are we getting a good return on our money?
- Are we on schedule with our deliveries?

The metrics identified and tracked will help leadership to confirm if true business value is delivered to business stakeholders (S. Ambler & Lines, 2012).

Summary:

Overall, when transitioning to an Agile methodology, there can be a culture clash between the old and new ways of working. This can lead to confusion and frustration among team members. Some team members may be resistant to the changes that are being made, particularly if they are comfortable with the old way of working. This can lead to conflict and slow down the transformation process. One of the biggest challenges during an Agile transformation is getting everyone on board with the new way of working. This includes understanding the principles of Agile, as well as the specific practices that will be used in the project. It can take time for everyone to fully understand and implement these changes. The transformation process is often time-consuming and can require a significant amount of effort from team members. This can lead to delays in the project timeline and missed deadlines. During an Agile transformation, there may be limited resources available to help with implementation, such as training materials or external consultants. This can make the process more difficult and slow down progress. It is important to recognize these challenges and plan ahead to ensure a successful Agile transformation. With proper planning and communication, it is possible to overcome these obstacles and reap the benefits of an Agile methodology.

3.2. Literature Review for Research Objective#2

In this section some concepts will be discussed related to research objective#2: Role of Agile Leadership & Agile Coach in Agile transformation.

3.2.1. Change of Leadership Role

Three crucial eras in the economic history of human civilization are the age of agriculture, the age of industry, and the age of the digital. Leadership styles from the agricultural era were inappropriate for the industrial era. Similarly, management from the industrial era does not apply to the digital era. Hence, a new kind of leadership is required in the age of digital age. A network of self-organizing teams led by a common objective are formed by the leadership of the digital age. This leadership approach necessitates a change in mindset, moving from an internal emphasis on outputs and efficiency to an external focus on customer value. To maximize people's potential, digital leadership uses innovation, collaboration, and compassion (Denning, 2021).

According to Ross (2020), the following changes best illustrate how the leadership role has changed in the digital age:

- Moving away from defining individual roles and toward allocating tasks with the greatest interest of the organization: this change signifies a departure from defining jobs and toward establishing missions. To achieve this, teams must be given clear missions that balance their individual autonomy.
- From decision-making to decision-facilitating: In the presence of accountable teams, conventional and hierarchical decision-making is constrained. Teams that are empowered accept responsibility for their actions and are better able to make choices that result in positive outcomes.
- From distributing resources to removing barriers: In their role as mini-CEOs, autonomous team leaders are fully in charge of the functionality, price, relationships with clients and partners, and life-cycle management. Organizations that choose to deploy autonomous teams become less concerned with

resource allocation and more concentrated on removing barriers that may stand in the way of success.

According to Mersino (2018), below tables contains the list of things that Agile leadership should stop doing and a list of things that Agile leadership should start doing.

Table 3. 1 Agile Leaders: Stop Doing & Start Doing

Stop Doing	Start Doing
Priorities shifting during the sprint	Do not change the priorities; instead, shield teams so they can concentrate. Learn about and support Agile roles.
Overriding the priorities established by the business owner for the team	Collaborate with the business world
Putting pressure on teams to meet unrealistic deadlines and accumulate technical debt	Set either dates or scope, but not both.
Taking people away from teams to work on special projects	Keep teams together.
Work overloading the team	Allow the team to work at their own pace.

Agile leadership is a type of transformative leadership that incorporates Emotional Intelligence (EI) to help teams navigate change and increase their effectiveness. Emotional Intelligence has been proven as a powerful tool for leaders to better understand the emotions and motivations of their teams, as well as to boost morale and foster trust. Emotional Intelligence is based on the premise that when individuals are able to better understand their emotions and others', they can build relationships, resolve conflicts, and make decisions with greater clarity. By understanding Emotional Intelligence and applying it in an Agile context, leaders can recognize potential issues before they become bigger problems. Moreover, Emotional Intelligence enables leaders to create an environment where creativity flourishes and collaboration is encouraged by understanding how each member contributes differently (Hayward, 2021).

Having Emotional Intelligence allows Agile leaders to motivate team members and foster strong relationships between them by finding common ground even in difficult situations. An effective Agile leader is able to recognize how team dynamics exist beyond individual contributions; rather, team atmosphere must be considered which requires an awareness of group feelings and reactions. Thus, Emotional Intelligence helps leaders proactively address emerging problems through communication strategies that are grounded in understanding human emotion rather than resorting right away to disciplinary action or punishment (Akkaya, 2020).

Agile Leaders have an in-depth understanding of the importance of Emotional Quotient (EQ), which is the ability to understand and manage one's emotions as well as the emotions of others. Emotional intelligence plays an important role in Agile leadership since it helps leaders empathize with their team members and better anticipate their needs. Agile Leaders are also knowledgeable about change management techniques since Agile projects are often met with resistance from team members due to their rapid pace and focus on instability. In addition to being well-versed in EQ and change management, Agile Leaders also possess strong organizational skills. This means they are able to effectively identify problems, plan solutions, allocate resources, prioritize tasks, delegate responsibilities, monitor progress, and adjust plans when necessary. These skills help them ensure that projects move forward smoothly while maintaining high standards of quality (Mdluli & Makhupe, 2017).

3.2.2. Agile Coaching

Coaching involves working together with clients in a stimulating and imaginative process that motivates them to realize their full potential on both a personal and professional level. A coach assists a learner or client in obtaining a personal or professional objective in this type of development. Agile coaches assist teams and organizations in maximizing individual gains. The role of the Agile coach should include: coach mentor; facilitator; teacher; conflict navigator; problem solver; and collaboration conductor. There are three common failure modes for an Agile coach: The coach becomes authoritarian and dictates how the team should work. This can kill the team's creativity and lead to resentment. Second, the coach becomes a doormat and does not provide the necessary guidance and support. This can lead to the team becoming stagnant or even failing. And finally, the coach becomes a cheerleader and fails to provide critical feedback. This can lead to the team becoming complacent and not improving. The best Agile coaches are those who are able to find the right balance between these three failure modes. They provide the team with the support and guidance they need, while also allowing them the freedom to be creative and innovative (Santos, et al, 2013).

The business world of today is continuously inundated with upheaval and unheard-of change. Because of this, it is particularly challenging for organizations to foresee potential opportunities and risks in the future. Organizations must completely embrace and integrate agility into their operations if they are to avoid this situation. However, priority must be given to Agile leadership for organizations to create a significant level of agility that is consistent with the current hypercompetitive and volatile market. Agile leaders and coaches may establish the guiding principles, create strategies, and create procedures that will facilitate an orderly transition to organizational agility (OA). These leaders provide guidance on how to make organizations Agile and make sure that the leadership culture in the organization models and support a comprehensive agility (Attar, & Abdul-Kareem, 2020).

Agile coaches are being introduced more frequently to assist Agile businesses advance quickly and achieve an advantage. Agile coaches provide services to teams and organizations. They have an impact on the Agile teams' effort, strategy, knowledge, and abilities. Being expressive, people-oriented, able to listen, diplomatic, and persistent are some of an Agile coach's most important qualities (Stray, Tkalich & Moe, 2020).

Agile coaching helps with the adoption, sustainability, and resolution of problems associated with that adoption. Software development teams and all other parties involved in the adoption of Agile are trained and developed with the assistance of Agile coaches. An Agile coach should have leadership abilities, project management skills, technical proficiency, and knowledge of Agile methodology. Agile coaches, with their extensive skill set, particularly their leadership abilities and traits, can play a significant role in addressing a number of challenges in Agile adoption, such as resistance to change, difficulty implementing Agile methods, removing obstacles to team autonomy in Agile teams, and improving the effectiveness of Agile meetings (Memon, 2020).

Agile coaching addresses obstacles to Agile adoption while facilitating the adoption and sustainability of Agile approaches. For instance, according to Stray, Memon & Paruch (2020), software development teams and all other parties involved in the adoption of Agile are trained and developed with the assistance of Agile coaches. The leadership traits, project management abilities, technical aptitude, and familiarity with Agile methodology are the core competencies of an Agile coach. It can be stated that Agile coaches are crucial in resolving issues like change resistance during an Agile transformation. In Agile teams, coaches put their attention on removing obstacles to team autonomy and enhancing the value of Agile meetings.

Corporate settings have acknowledged the value of Agile coaches in the use of Agile principles. An Agile coach focuses on maximizing people's potential and using it to produce worthwhile outcomes more quickly. A coach is generally an itinerant person who can build anything from team structure to system architecture in addition to observing, mentoring, negotiating, and leading (Fraser et al, 2009).

Summary:

Overall, Agile Leaders & Coaches must be able to motivate their teams through periods of change by creating a sense of ownership and commitment to the project objectives. They do this by setting clear expectations, engaging in frequent communication, giving frequent feedback, and creating recognition opportunities for team members who excel at meeting goals. Agile Leadership & Coaching requires a deep understanding of the human side of business – things like motivation, culture development, communication styles, goal setting strategies – all of which contribute to successful project completion. Agile Leaders & Coaches must be adept at inspiring both the individuals on their teams as well as the entire organization itself – leading by example with integrity and adaptability.

3.3. Literature Review for Research Objective#3

In this section some concepts will be discussed related to research objective#3: Identify the techniques to sustain as Agile enterprise.

3.3.1. Innovation and Adoption

Innovation involves more than just coming up with the organization's next big idea. It also involves how you put into practice the ideas that are generated and successfully utilized, as well as how you establish the culture that will enable you to continue generating new ideas. A number of techniques facilitate the ongoing adaptation and use of innovation. The following are the three techniques where the role of technology leaders in their implementation will be examined (MJV Technology and Innovation, 2019):

1) **Design Thinking**: Design Thinking is used to enhance end-user comprehension. In order to foster empathy, this approach aims to research user behavior, wants, and desires. A company

can then outline the demand and offer proactive solutions that will be prototyped and assessed before being put into action.

2) **Lean Startup**: Lean Startup is a group of techniques intended to thoroughly evaluate recently developed technologies. In order to preserve the hypothesis of innovation without wasting time or money, it is vital to do so.
3) **Agile Scrum**: This methodology enables the adoption of a solution across the firm while taking into account internal IT decisions, corporate governance, and other factors and gaining the advantages of Agile approaches.

According to Olteanu (2018), training and workshops, the involvement of Agile specialists, support and effectiveness, the development of community practice, and understanding corporate culture are some of the most crucial prerequisites for Agile transformation. However, the most Agile issue for firms undergoing transformation is the never-ending learning process that is a component of the learning organizational culture. This transformation is like a trip without a destination because it requires constant adaptation to changes.

Innovation, which is best described as the profitable application of creativity, constantly strives to provide ground-breaking answers to significant client problems and to do it in an efficient manner. Design and development are involved, and they need to be seamlessly integrated and quickly modified to match the direction and velocity of market changes. Precisely that is what Agile accomplishes (Rigby, Berez, Caimi & Noble, 2015).

The innovation process can benefit from agile approaches because of the many ways in which they improve organizational processes, the sharing of knowledge and insights, and the identification and understanding of customer demands. Some of the Agile guidelines for leaders and project team members to improve the innovation process include the use of simple user stories as a solution for the lengthy documentation, eliminate fixed implementations plans in order to improve an incremental product development process, using, for example, war rooms to accommodate the transfer of knowledge and know-how, and integrating the fuzzy front end to the whole process of coming up with new ideas, which is done in loops with customer participation (Hannola, Friman, & Niemimuukko, 2013).

The company must first be adaptable if it is to be able to be Agile. It takes a lot of effort for people to change their behavior and break old patterns. Therefore, it is critical to have management permission to take chances with little risk to the individual (Findsrud, 2020).

Developing the Agile mindset within the enterprise can help sustain enterprise agility. The Disciplined Agile mindset promises, according to Ambler and Lines (2020), are agreements made with coworkers, stakeholders, and other individuals with whom we interact on a daily basis.

- Help people feel safe and accept that people are different.
- Speed up the rate at which value is created.
- Work together and do things.
- Make your work and workflow clear.
- Make things more predictable.
- Do not take on more than you can handle.
- Continue improving.

The promises outlined above are set of disciplined actions that help team to work well together and in a professional way in order to develop Agile mindset and sustain Agility (Ambler & Lines 2020).

3.3.2. Agile Metrics

Agile metrics is way to inspect the Agile practice in enterprise, take appropriate actions to sustain enterprise agility. According to AgilityHealth (2022), Performance, Agile Leadership, Agile Culture, Core Values, and Team Clarity are all measured by means of online forms on the Agility Health Radar. The employees are required to fill out various online questionnaires in order for any information to be gathered. The findings of the analysis are then made available in a PDF format by Agility Health, the company that developed the instrument. The analysis is carried out with the assistance of artificial intelligence. The most important role that the tool plays for companies is to play a part in the teams' and organizations' efforts to reach their full potential.

Figure 3. 2 Sample of Health Radar Report

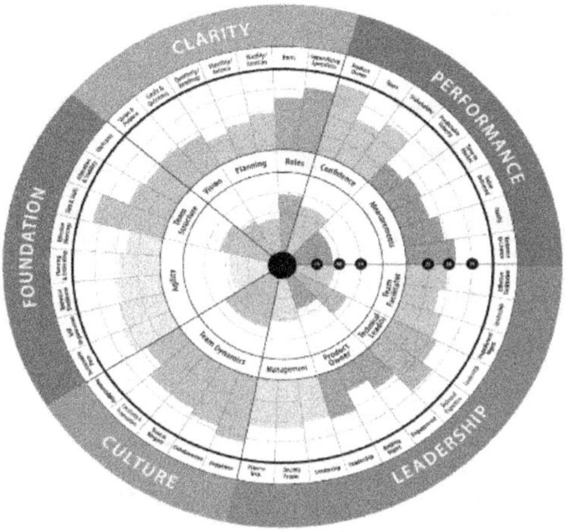

Source: https://agilityhealthradar.com

Agility Heatlh Radar provides several types of radars, these types of radars will help organization to measure, grow and sustain Agility in the enterprise: TeamHealth Radar, TeamCulture Radar, DevOps Health Radar, Lean Product Health Radar, Program Health Radar, Enterprise Business Agility Health Radar, Digital Transformation Radar, Lean Portfolio Health Radar, Agile Talent & HR Health Radar, Enterprise Business Agility Strategist Radar, Agile Team Coach Radar, Leadership Agility Radar, Product Owner Radar and Scrum Master Radar (AgilityHealth, 2022).

On top of the above, Agility heath radar also provides framework specific health radars. For example, SAFe health radars help to assess the SAFe framework maturity of an organization and sustain Agility: SAFe® Team and Technical Agility Health Radar, SAFe® business Agility Health Radar, SAFe® Lean Portfolio Management Health Radar, SAFe® Agile Product Delivery Health Radar, SAFe® DevOps Health Radar, SAFe® Organizational Agility Health Radar and SAFe® Release Train Engineer Radar (AgilityHealth, 2022).

As stated by Axelos (2017), the Agilometer is applied to the task of analyzing significant aspects of the project, sample Agilometer shown in below figure.

Figure 3. 3 Sample of Agilometer

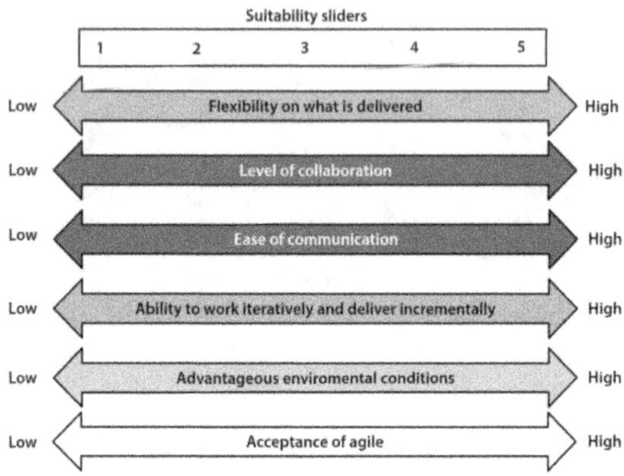

Source: AXELOS Limited 2017

Agilometer provides a good idea of how successful working Agile may be for a particular project or how the project can adjust to make Agile more suited. When assessing a project, Agile does not consider it to be "Agile" or "not Agile;" rather, it assesses the project based on the degree to which it can adopt Agile. The Agilometer is a tool that can be utilized to validate the level of Agile that has been put into practice. Instead of representing actual scores, the values on the slider (1: low to 5: high) are merely indicative and are meant to point out potential areas for improvement. After that, the data are put to use in order to identify risk areas that can either be eliminated or reduced in order to sustain Agility (Axelos, 2017, pp31-32).

Summary:

Agile Innovation and Adaptation allows developers to quickly respond to customer demands, iterate on existing products and platforms, and launch new features in a timely manner. By focusing on rapid iterations of the product development process, teams can ensure that their solutions remain up-to-date and relevant for customers. Agile Innovation and Adaptation also encourages collaboration among different stakeholders, allowing them to come up with creative solutions that take into account the needs of everyone involved. By utilizing this approach, companies can ensure that their products are constantly evolving in order to meet the changing demands of customers and markets. Ultimately, Agile Innovation and Adaptation helps businesses innovate faster while still maintaining high quality results. Similarly, Agile mindset, inspecting though metrics and continuous improvement will help organizations to sustain Agility.

3.4. Literature Review for Research Objective#4

In this section some concepts will be discussed related to research objective#4: Role of Agile methodologies in business & digital transformation of IT companies.

3.4.1. Role of Agile in Business & Digital Transformation

According to the research done by Fachrunnisa, Adhiatma, Lukman, & Ab Majid (2020), the implementation of digital transformation depends on Agile leadership. The establishment of digital transformation in SMEs is further influenced by the strategic flexibility that results from workforce transformation and dynamic capabilities. The effectiveness of implementing digital transformation depends greatly on the leader's quick response time and flexibility of approach.

According to Kapitsaki & Christou (2015), since software engineering first made an official appearance, software processes have seen tremendous evolution. Academics and business leaders have created, accepted, or rejected a number of approaches that, in principle or in practice, are more or less effective. Agile approaches, widely used in the past ten years, are currently a trend. It is essential to monitor the evolution of software processes throughout time because they are always changing.

As stated by Sánchez (2017), the transition from the industrial period to the era of intelligent and connected devices has had a significant impact on organizations and competition. Digital technologies are causing an organizational shift (social, mobile, big data, cloud computing, Internet of Things). Even in industries that do not use information extensively, like agriculture or mining, the impact of information technology is significant. The global supply chain procedures, leadership, data governance, and how to integrate technologies to alter the business are just a few of the problems that the digital transformation poses. These obstacles could be of a size and nature that was unthinkable decades ago. Traditional business models are put to the test by this transformation.

According to Guruswamy, Adikari & Srinivasaraghavan (2016), businesses must reevaluate their customers' needs to a larger level and go through digital transformation to compete in the market as a result of the rising demand for mobile and internet applications. Agile methodologies are becoming more and more popular as a strategy for creating creative solutions, while Design Thinking fosters transformation, evolution, and innovation as well as the creation of fresh approaches to managing both present and future company prospects.

As per research done by Bresciani, Ferraris, Romano & Santoro (2021), the company's use of technologies is just one aspect of transformation; other aspects include strategies, activities, processes, skills, competencies, revenue models, and expenses. All of these factors call for academic study and have significant consequences for how digitalization ought to be accepted. Digital technology investments are rising across numerous industries. Such investments enable the creation of new competitive advantages connected to cost reduction via improved efficiency and revenue growth through the creation of novel business models or products.

As stated by Parsons, Ryu, & Lal (2007), without significantly raising project costs, Agile methodologies do indeed improve the quality, satisfaction, and productivity of software development project outputs. The usage of numerous ways in combination and the adoption of sets of techniques on an as-needed basis, however, seem to indicate that method adoption involves a high degree of adaptivity.

Participation in the 15th State of Agile survey, which was sponsored by digital.ai and held between February and April 2021, was open to members of the global software development communities from a diverse set of industries. The total number of responses was 4,182, with 1,382 complete surveys being collected, analyzed, and compiled into a report for presentation. The depiction of the survey results concerning the advantages of adopting an Agile methodology can be found below (State of Agile, 2021).

Figure 3. 4 Fifteenth State of Agile Survey

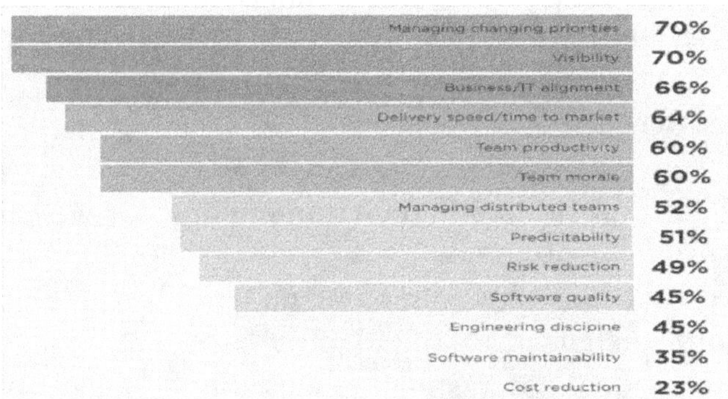

Source: State of Agile

As shown in the above figure, both business and IT alignment as well as visibility across all Agile teams were determined to be essential components of an effective Agile adoption strategy. Two thirds of respondents believe that the adoption of Agile approaches has the greatest positive impact on management, visibility, and alignment (State of Agile, 2021).

According Axelos (2017, pp 11), Agile provides enterprises with their need to success in the current environment, including learn early, risk reduction, and benefits of quick delivery.

These advantages can be gained by implementing Agile practices. When a difficult problem is broken down into more manageable pieces, it is much easier to obtain timely feedback from customers and, as a result, to keep moving forward. When things are smaller, they progress more quickly, and it is easy to make a many small chunks in order to gain confidence in stakeholders and deliver solution stakeholders needed. The capacity to experience setbacks in a short amount of time is essential to this. If you suspect that you are heading in the wrong direction, you should ascertain this reality as soon as you possibly can. It is possible that the difference between success and failure will be determined by whether a portion or the majority of what was required was delivered early or whether all of it was delivered at a later date.

According to S. Ambler & Lines (2012), DAD (Disciplined Agile Delivery) takes a goal-driven approach. As it is defined by DAD, the goal is where we want to end up. There are several benefits of goal-driven approach as below:

- Goals offer us remain focused
- Goals help motivated
- Goals are a useful tool for determining how far we have come (measuring the progress)
- Setting goals keeps us committed and prevents us from becoming distracted.
- Able to conquer procrastination with the assistance of goals.

Thence, goal-driven approach helps in successful business and digital transformation keeping goal is a focus point (S. Ambler & Lines, 2012).

Summary:

Agile methodologies have become a popular approach in helping organizations design, develop, and deliver high-quality digital applications and services. By implementing agile principles, teams can identify customer needs faster and adjust their product or service accordingly. This helps the businesses in the IT industry in staying competitive, quickly adapt and innovate in order to get succeeded in business and digital transformation.

3.5. Literature Review for Research Objective#5

In this section some concepts will be discussed related to research objective#5: Agile adaption in IT organizations foster business agility and overcome the digital transformation challenges.

3.5.1. Business Agility

For businesses today, agility is essential in order to stay ahead of the competition. Companies must be able to react quickly and strategically as customer needs change, new technologies emerge, and new competitors enter the market. This requires a shift from traditional modes of business operations towards more dynamic and flexible ones.

Business agility involves developing an Agile mindset where employees are encouraged to think creatively about how the organization can improve processes, products and services for customers. Organizations should focus on creating a culture that values innovation and collaboration between teams. This allows organizations to put into place effective strategies that enable them to respond quickly when customer requirements or competitive pressures arise (Osmundsen, Iden & Bygstad, 2018).

According to Kotter (2014), Management is the process of Planning, Budgeting, Organizing, Staffing, Measuring, Problem Solving, Doing what we know how to do exceptionally well and producing reliable, dependable results constantly while Leadership is the process of establishing direction, aligning people, motivating, inspiring, mobilizing people to achieve astonishing results and propelling the employees into the future.

As stated by Almeida, Oliveira & Neves (2022), a management approach known as "Management 3.0" aims to be in line with collaborative and digital developments. Disruptive technologies and quickening digitization processes pose a persistent threat to traditional businesses. The ongoing need for innovation presents a number of difficulties for business expansion, team morale, and quick decision-making. To address such complicated difficulties, businesses are reevaluating their management models and giving up traditional management techniques. Agile approaches, which were originally developed for software engineering, are now being used in organizational management.

According to Zaydi & Nassereddine (2020), the continuous delivery of information technology (IT) services enabled by development operations (DevOps) is problematic if security best practices are not properly taken into account. On the other hand, if security is integrated into the continuous delivery pipeline in accordance with best practices, Security Operations (SecOps) has the potential to reduce security risks. Before incorporating these principles into their IT Service Management, organizations require a foundation for comprehending the DevSecOps culture.

3.5.2. Digital Transformation Challenges

Business agility is a set of capabilities, behaviors, and ways of working that allow your company to achieve its goals with more freedom, flexibility, and resilience. Despite the future. Business Agility helps to eliminate digital transformation VUCA challenges. A volatile, uncertain, complex, and ambiguous (VUCA) environment has a substantial impact on business operations, necessitating the agility of businesses to maintain a competitive edge. To adapt and operate in a VUCA environment, businesses require new skill sets and technologies, as well as innovation and the usage of Agile frameworks (Talik, 2021). The COVID-19 pandemic is an illustration of a VUCA situation that continues to impact how many firms execute and respond to digital transformation. In a VUCA world, business agility should be the new operating model for Agile organizations. The defining cultural and behavioral traits of an Agile organization are represented by the Domains of Business Agility (Leadership, Individuals, and Operations) in the figure below (Business Agility Institute, n.d.).

Figure 3. 5 Domains of Business Agility

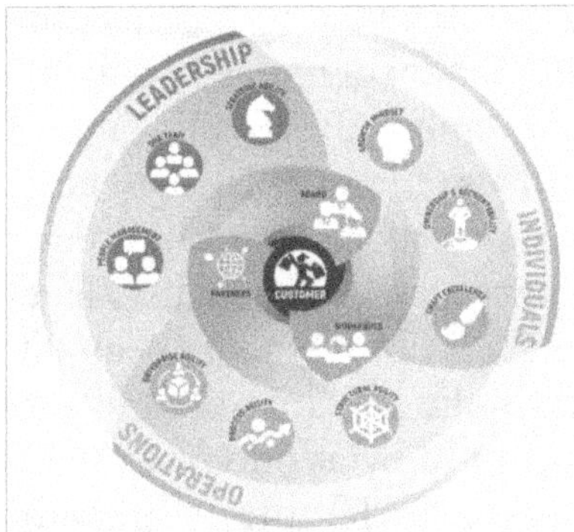

Source: https://businessagility.institute/

Over the course of the entire organizational system, each area is equally necessary, important, and interdependent. This model illustrates the skills necessary for a company to nimbly seize new and unanticipated opportunities for the benefit of its clients. The Domains of Business Agility serve as a useful road map for every phase of the transformation procedure, from start to finish (Business Agility Institute, n.d.).

One of the fuller approach Agile methodologies named SAFe (Scaled Agile Framework conducted survey to understand the benefits of scaling Agile with SAFe, the participants around 1 million working on 20K organizations around the globe have agreed the benefits of scaling Agile with SAFe. Below is the summary of results (Scaled Agile, Inc, 2022):

Figure 3. 6 SAFe Survey Results

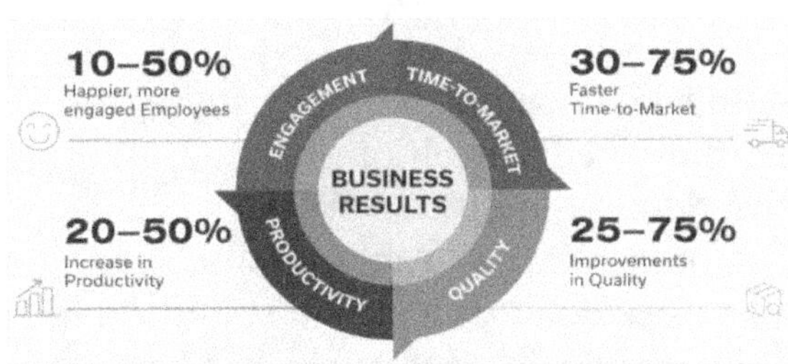

Source: Scaled Agile, Inc, 2022

Time to Market, one of the advantages of expanding Agile with SAFe is a reduction in time-to-market. By uniting Agile cross-functional teams around value, leading organizations can meet consumer demands more quickly, time to market increased by 75%. Scaled Agile Framework enables them to make speedier choices, communicate more effectively, improve operations, and maintain customer focus. **Quality Improvement**, built-in quality is one of the key SAFe ideals, highlighting the importance of integrating quality into each phase of the development cycle and achieving up to a 75% improvement in quality. In this manner, growing Agile with SAFe rewards organizations by shifting the responsibility of quality to everyone from the last-moment focus. **Productivity Increase**, SAFe offers quantifiable productivity increases of up to 50% by enabling top-performing teams and teams of teams to eliminate wasteful tasks, identify and fix delays, constantly improve, and ensure they are creating the correct things. **Employee Engagement**, happy and engaged workers are more productive. Expanding Agile with the Scaled Agile Framework (SAFe) can help knowledge workers achieve autonomy, mastery, and purpose, the basic ingredients in unlocking intrinsic motivation. Through the use of SAFe, businesses have the tools to cut down on burnout, promote morale, and raise engagement levels by as much as 50% (Scaled Agile, Inc, 2022).

3.5.3. Look of Agile in Some Organizations

In this section we will discuss about benefits gained by some organization by overcoming digital transformation challenges with Agile adoption.

1. Starbucks

Starbucks is one of the most successful companies in the world, and they credit much of their success to their adoption of Agile methodology. In 2015, Starbucks decided to switch from a waterfall approach to an Agile approach in order to be more responsive to customer needs. The results have been impressive. Since making the switch, Starbucks has been able to roll out new features and products much more quickly and efficiently. As a result, they have been able to better meet the needs of their customers and stay ahead of the competition (Grusendorf, 2017).

2. Adobe

Adobe is another company that has seen great success with Agile methodology. In 2016, Adobe switched from a traditional approach to Agile in order to speed up their product development cycle. The results have been impressive. Adobe has been able to increase its release frequency by 400%, which has helped them gain a competitive edge in the market. In addition, they have seen increased employee satisfaction and engagement since making the switch (Green, 2012).

3. Spotify

Spotify is yet another company that has benefitted greatly from adopting an Agile approach. Spotify switched to Agile in 2015 in order to speed up product development cycle and better respond to customer needs. Since making the switch, Spotify has been able release new features much more quickly than before. In addition, they have seen increased employee satisfaction and engagement since making the switch (Alqudah & Razali, 2016).

Summary:

In order for organizations to achieve agility, they need a systematic approach that incorporates both strategy and technology. This requires investment in technology such as automation tools that will allow companies to swiftly adjust processes and scale operations according to changing circumstances. It also involves using data-driven insights in order to determine what activities should be focused on most in order for businesses to remain competitive in their respective markets.

Ultimately, business agility is key for companies who want remain relevant in an ever-changing market landscape. By having the ability to quickly adjust operations while still providing exceptional customer service organizations can ensure they continue to successfully meet customer needs and stay ahead of their competition.

CHAPTER 4

4. RESEARCH METHODOLOGY

4.1. Research Design

Research Design is a systematic approach to planning and conducting research. It involves the identification of a problem or question, the development of a research plan to address that problem or question, the collection and analysis of data to answer the research question, and the interpretation of the results.

For this research, as a first step problem has been identified. Later formulated the research objectives, research questions and null hypothesize are identified (described in chapter#1). Research objectives served to formulate the theoretical framework and review the existing literature. Research questions are helpful to identify the secondary data collection questionnaire. Hypothesizes are useful to confirm to what extent Agile adoption, Agile leadership and Agile coach roles are helpful in organization Agile transformation, business and digital transformation.

Survey questionnaire is sent to several IT professionals to collect their opinions as a secondary data. To analyze the secondary data quantitative data analysis is considered is best because of affordability, efficiency and easy to derive conclusions (Creswell, 2003).

Qualitative research is often used to explore new topics or to gain a better understanding of complex phenomena. This type of research is usually exploratory in nature and relies heavily on data that is collected through interviews, focus groups, or observations. Qualitative research is often seen as more subjective than quantitative research because it relies heavily on the researcher's interpretation of the data (Creswell, 2003).

Quantitative research, on the other hand, is typically used to test hypotheses or to compare two or more groups. This type of research relies heavily on data that is collected through surveys or experiments. Quantitative research is often seen as more objective than qualitative research because it is less reliant on the researcher's interpretation of the data (Creswell, 2003). Hence, quantitative analysis is considered best for this research.

4.2. Web-Based Survey

For this research, web-based survey is used. A web-based survey is a type of survey that is conducted online. This type of survey has many advantages over other types of surveys, such as paper-based surveys. Some of the advantages of web-based surveys include (Solomon, 2000):

- They are less expensive to administer than paper-based surveys.
- They are more convenient for respondents, as they can be taken at any time and from any location with an internet connection.
- They allow for real-time data collection and analysis.
- They offer a greater degree of anonymity for respondents, which can lead to higher quality data.

Google forms is the tool used to conduct the web-based survey. This survey is sent via email, LinkedIn, WhatsApp groups to professionals working in IT (Information Technology) and ITeS (IT enabled Services) companies.

4.3. Population and Sample

A population refers to all individuals in a defined group, while a sample is a smaller, representative subset of that population. In research, populations are often very large, making it impractical or impossible to study every individual. Sampling allows researchers to study a smaller group that is still representative of the larger population. For this research survey responses from 160 professionals are used.

4.4. Tools Used in Data Analysis

Most popular statistical analysis tool i.e., SPSS ver.29 is used to conduct the quantitative data analysis on survey responses (secondary data). Following are the statistical analysis were conducted using SPSS ver.29: Reliability Measure, Mean, Standard Deviation, Variance, Correlation Analysis and Linear Regression. In chapter#5 these data analyses are explained in detail.

CHAPTER 5

5. DATA ANALYSIS & INTERPRETATION

5.1 Demographics of Survey Respondents

Below are the demographic details of survey respondents.

5.1.1 Gender of Respondents

Table 5. 1 Gender of Respondents

No.	Option	Frequency	Percentage (%)
1	Male	119	74.38%
2	Female	41	25.63%
	Total	160	100%

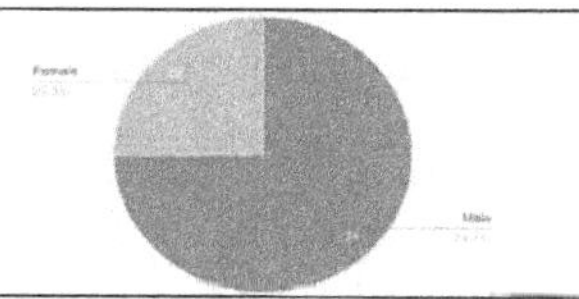

Inference: Around 26% of the respondents participated in the survey are male while about 74% of them are female.

5.1.2 Age Group of Respondents

Table 5. 2 Age of Respondents

No.	Option	Frequency	Percentage
1	Less than 30 Years	8	5.00%
2	30 to 40 Years	70	43.75%
3	40 to 50 Years	70	43.75%
4	More than 50 Years	12	7.50%
	Total	160	100%

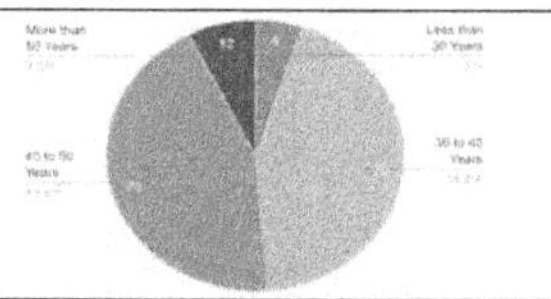

Inference: 5% of the respondents surveyed are less than 30 years while about 44% are in the age group of 30 to 40 years. Another 44% of the respondents are in the age group of 40 to 50 years and the remaining 7% of the respondents are above 50 years.

5.1.3 Sector of Respondents

Table 5. 3 Sector of Respondents

No.	Option	Frequency	Percentage
1	IT	160	100%
2	Non-IT	0	0%
	Total	160	100%

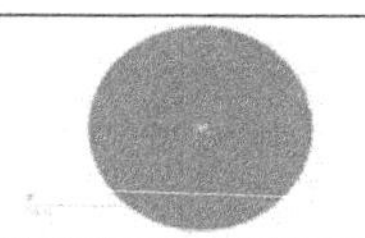

Inference: All the 100% of the respondents surveyed are from IT sector. Agile Technologies are popularly used in IT Companies compared to the other sectors.

5.1.4 Region of Respondents

Table 5. 4 Region of Respondents

No.	Option	Frequency	Percentage
1	Asia Pacific	36	22.50%
2	Americas	48	30.00%
3	Europe	53	33.13%
4	Middle East /Africa	23	14.38%
	Total	160	100%

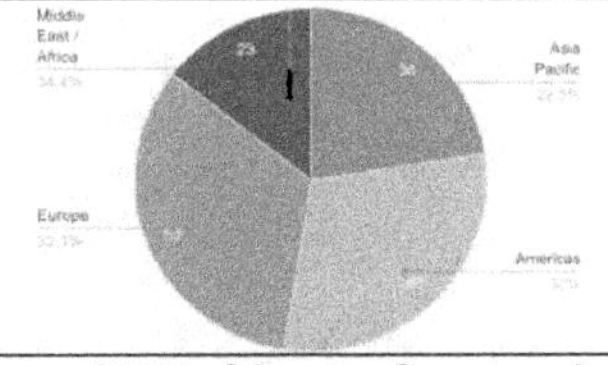

Inference: 33% of the respondents surveyed are from Europe and 30% of them are from Americas. 22% of the respondents are from Asia Pacific while the remaining 14% are from Middle East and Africa.

5.1.5 Job Experience of Respondents

Table 5. 5 Job Experience of Respondents

No.	Option	Frequency	Percentage
1	Less than a year	0	0%
2	2 to 3 years	1	0.63%
3	3 to 5 years	36	22.50%
4	More than 5 years	123	76.88%
	Total	160	100%

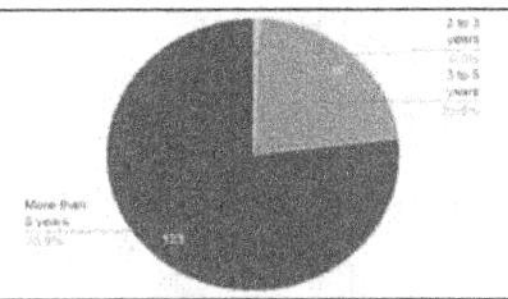

Inference: Around 77% of the respondents have job experience of more than 5 years while 22% of the respondents have an experience between 3 to 5 years. Only one respondent has an experience between 2 to 3 years.

5.1.6 Respondents Participation in Agile Transformation

Table 5. 6 Respondents Participation in Agile Transformation

No.	Option	Frequency	Percentage (%)
1	Yes	154	96.25%
2	No	6	3.75%
	Total	160	100%

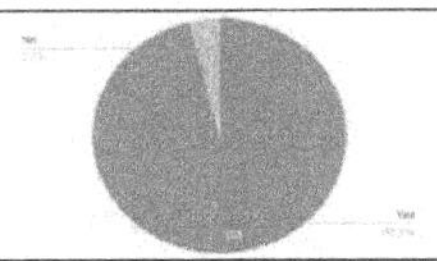

Inference: 96% of the respondents have the experience of participating in Agile Transformation and the remaining 4% of the respondents do not have the experience.

5.1.7 Organization Culture of Respondents

Table 5. 7 Organization Culture of Respondents

No.	Option	Frequency	Percentage
1	Self-Designing	11	6.88%
2	Self-Governance	13	8.13%
3	Led by Manager	12	7.50%
4	Self-organizing and self-managing	124	77.5%
	Total	160	100%

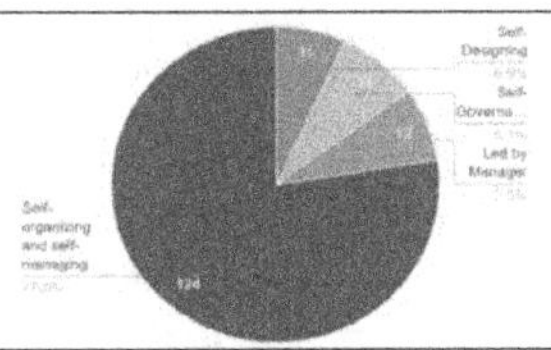

Inference: 77% of the respondents follow self-organizing and self-managing organization culture while 8% of the respondents follow self-governance. 8% of the respondents are led by manager and the remaining 7% follow the self-designing culture mode.

5.1.8 Experience of Company in practicing Agile

Table 5. 8 Agile Experience of Organization

No.	Option	Frequency	Percentage
1	Less than a year	0	0%
2	2 to 3 years	0	0%
3	3 to 5 years	37	23.13%
4	More than 5 years	123	76.88%
	Total	160	100%

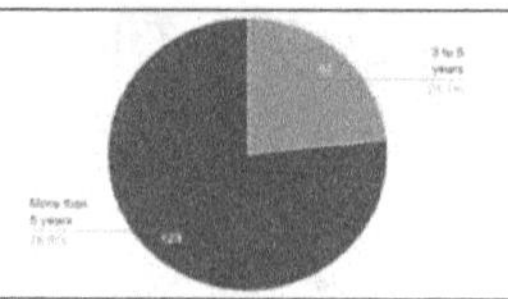

Inference: 77% of the companies where the respondents are working have an experience of more than 5 years in practicing Agile while the remaining 23% have 3 to 5 years' experience.

5.1.9 Designation of Respondents

Table 5. 9 Designation of Respondents

No.	Option	Frequency	Percentage
1	Project/Program Manager	12	7.50%
2	Team Leader/Architect	14	8.75%
3	Vice President/Management or Executive Leadership	16	10.00%
4	Business Analyst/Business Manager/Product Manager/Product Owner	22	13.75%
5	Scrum Master/Agile Coach/Agile Transformation Consultant	96	60.00%
	Total	160	100%

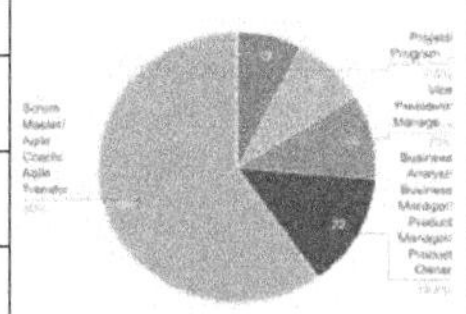

Inference: Majority of the respondents in the survey include Scrum Master/Agile Coach/Agile Transformation Consultant (60%) followed by Business Analyst/Business Manager/Product Manager/Product Owner (13.75%). Other respondents include Vice President/Management or Executive Leadership (10%), Team Leader/Architect (8.75%), Project/Program Manager (7.50%).

5.2 Results of Survey Questionnaire

Below are descriptive statistical survey results for each survey question related to each of the hypothesis.

5.2.1. Survey Results for Hypothesis#1

Hypothesis#1: Overcoming Agile adoption challenges is not important to implement Agile and transform as an Agile Enterprise.

Table 5. 10 Results of Survey Statement#1

Survey Statement#1: Agile transformation in an organization is influenced by the support of its leadership team.

No.	Option	Frequency	Percentage
1	Strongly Agree	90	56.25%
2	Agree	70	43.75%
3	Neutral	0	0%
4	Disagree	0	0%
5	Strongly Disagree	0	0%
	Total	160	100%

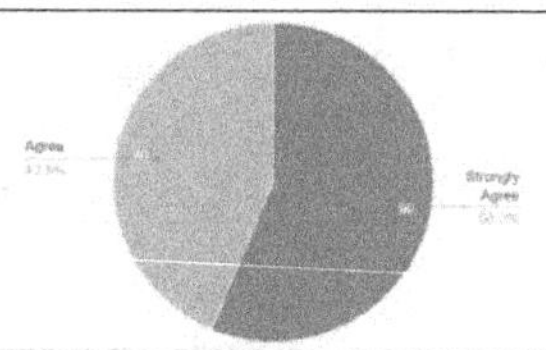

Inference: 56% of the respondents strongly agree and another 44% of the respondents agree that Agile transformation in an organization is influenced by the support of its leadership team. Leadership is a key factor in determining the success of Agile transformation; this was clearly evident, with an impressive 100% of respondents showing agreement on the matter.

Table 5. 11 Results of Survey Statement#2

Survey Statement#2: Inter-team communication plays no role in an organization's Agile transformation.

No.	Option	Frequency	Percentage
1	Strongly Agree	0	0%
2	Agree	0	0%
3	Neutral	0	0%
4	Disagree	90	56.25%
5	Strongly Disagree	70	43.75%
	Total	**160**	**100%**

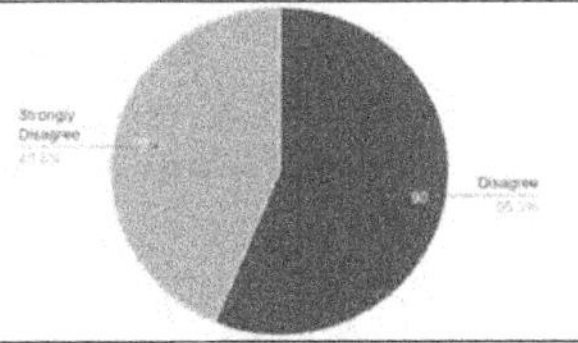

Inference: 56% of the respondents disagree and another 44% of the respondents strongly disagree that Inter-team communication plays no role in an organization's Agile transformation. An overwhelming majority of the total respondents feel that Inter-team communication is an essential factor in driving successful Agile transformations. Clearly this suggests a strong need for further focus on clear dialogue and cooperation between teams involved.

Table 5. 12 Results of Survey Statement#3

Survey Statement#3: Failure to invest in talent impedes the successful implementation of Agile.

No.	Option	Frequency	Percentage
1	Strongly Agree	68	42.50%
2	Agree	92	57.50%
3	Neutral	0	0%
4	Disagree	0	0%
5	Strongly Disagree	0	0%
	Total	**160**	**100%**

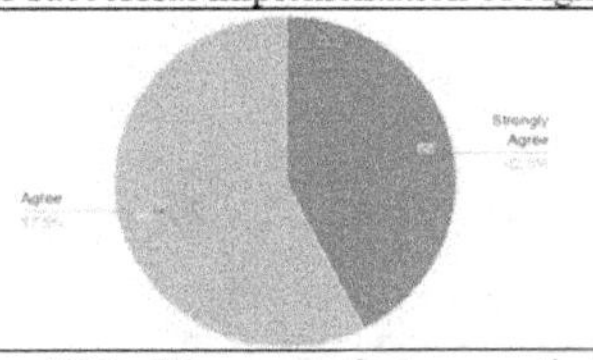

Inference: 42% of the respondents strongly agree and another 57% of the respondents agree that failure to invest in talent impedes the successful transformation of Agile. An overwhelming majority of survey respondents recognize the pivotal role talent investment plays in successful Agile transformation and failure to invest can be a major impediment.

Table 5. 13 Results of Survey Statement#4

Survey Statement#4: Unclear organizational structure (roles and responsibilities) hinders Agile transformation.

No.	Option	Frequency	Percentage
1	Strongly Agree	57	35.63%
2	Agree	103	64.38%
3	Neutral	0	0%
4	Disagree	0	0%
5	Strongly Disagree	0	0%
	Total	**160**	**100%**

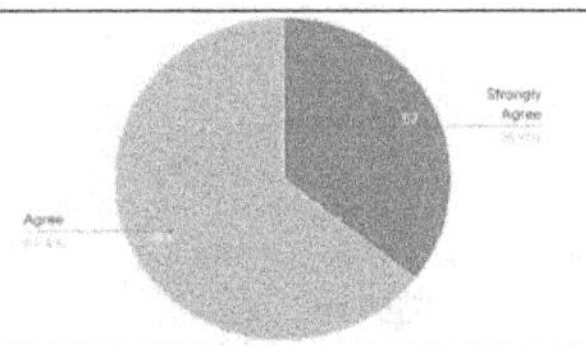

Inference: 36% of the respondents strongly agree and another 64% of the respondents agree that unclear organizational structure (roles and responsibilities) hinders Agile transformation. Survey results indicate a strong consensus that ambiguity surrounding roles and responsibilities negatively impacts successful Agile transformation.

Table 5. 14 Results of Survey Statement#5

Survey Statement#5: Right tools are essential for a successful Agile transformation			
No.	**Option**	**Frequency**	**Percentage**
1	Strongly Agree	48	30.00%
2	Agree	111	69.38%
3	Neutral	1	0.63%
4	Disagree	0	0%
5	Strongly Disagree	0	0%
	Total	**160**	**100%**

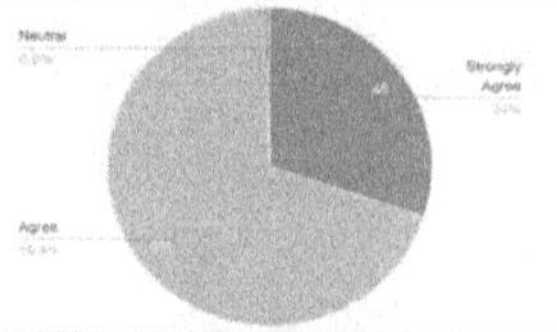

Inference: An overwhelming majority of respondents recognize the importance of having the right tools for a successful Agile transformation. Almost 30% held firmly to this belief and an additional 69% agreed, underscoring its significance in achieving success.

Table 5. 15 Results of Survey Statement#6

Survey Statement#6: Employee's resistance to culture shift can be a challenge in Agile transformation			
No.	**Option**	**Frequency**	**Percentage**
1	Strongly Agree	84	52.50%
2	Agree	76	47.50%
3	Neutral	0	0%
4	Disagree	0	0%
5	Strongly Disagree	0	0%
	Total	**160**	**100%**

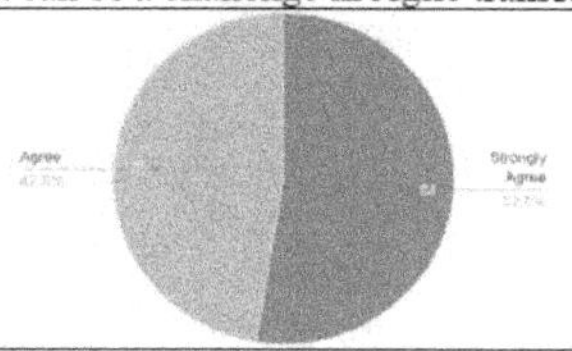

Inference: 52% of the respondents strongly agree and another 48% of the respondents agree that Employee's resistance to culture shift can be a challenge in Agile transformation. A decisive majority of respondents concurred that transitioning to an Agile environment can be a formidable challenge due to employee resistance.

Table 5. 16 Results of Survey Statement#7

Survey Statement#7: Agile transformation is not hampered by improperly applying Agile techniques			
No.	**Option**	**Frequency**	**Percentage**
1	Strongly Agree	0	0%
2	Agree	0	0%
3	Neutral	0	0%
4	Disagree	74	46.25%
5	Strongly Disagree	86	53.75%
	Total	**160**	**100%**

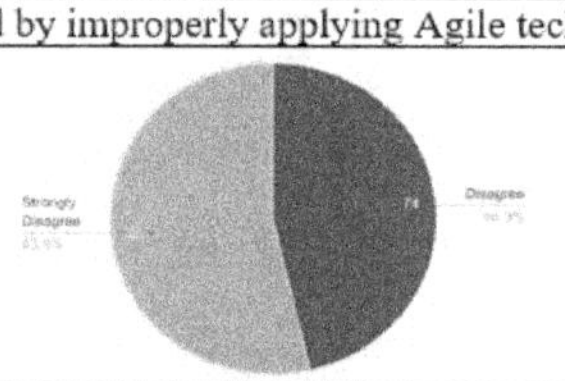

Inference: 46% of the respondents disagree and another 54% of the respondents strongly disagree that Agile transformation is not hampered by improperly applying Agile techniques. It is evident that many believe proper application of Agile principles leads to success in its adoption and use.

5.2.2. Survey Results for Hypothesis#2

Hypothesis#2: Agile Leadership and Agile Coaching are not critical success factors in adopting Agile & transformation in IT Companies.

Table 5. 17 Results of Survey Statement#8

Survey Statement#8: Agile Leadership should clearly communicate the compelling change vision and exhibit openness to an Agile way of working

No.	Option	Frequency	Percentage
1	Strongly Agree	80	50%
2	Agree	80	50%
3	Neutral	0	0%
4	Disagree	0	0%
5	Strongly Disagree	0	0%
	Total	**160**	**100%**

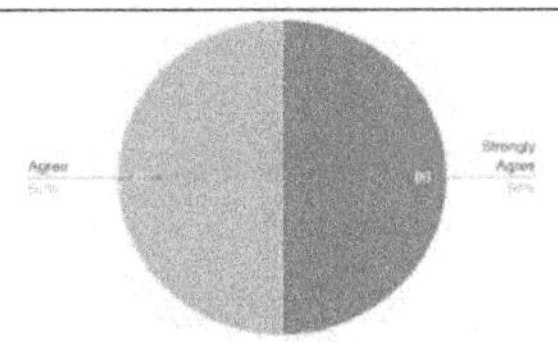

Inference: 50% of the respondents strongly agree and another 50% of the respondents agree that Agile Leadership should clearly communicate the compelling change vision and exhibit openness to an Agile way of working. This implies that that Agile Leadership requires well-defined communication around the change vision and openness to an Agile approach in order for it to be successful.

Table 5. 18 Results of Survey Statement#9

Survey Statement#9: Agile leaders do not have to lead by example and authenticity

No.	Option	Frequency	Percentage
1	Strongly Agree	0	0%
2	Agree	0	0%
3	Neutral	0	0%
4	Disagree	67	41.88%
5	Strongly Disagree	93	58.13%
	Total	**160**	**100%**

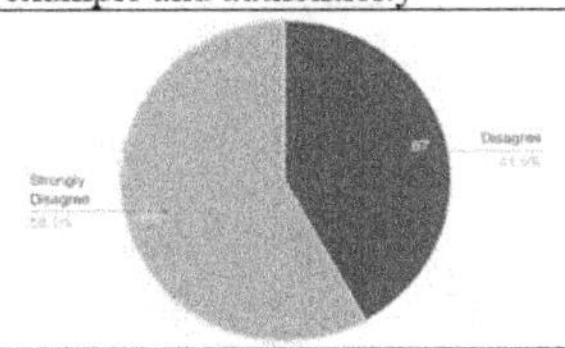

Inference: A majority of survey respondents - 100%! - disagree that Agile leaders do not need to lead with authenticity and example-setting. This strong consensus highlights the importance of Agile leadership leading for successful Agile transformation.

Table 5. 19 Results of Survey Statement#10

Survey Statement#10: Agile leaders should transfer the decision-making authority to where the information is available (known as decentralized decision making)

No.	Option	Frequency	Percentage
1	Strongly Agree	59	36.88%
2	Agree	101	63.13%
3	Neutral	0	0%
4	Disagree	0	0%
5	Strongly Disagree	0	0%
	Total	**160**	**100%**

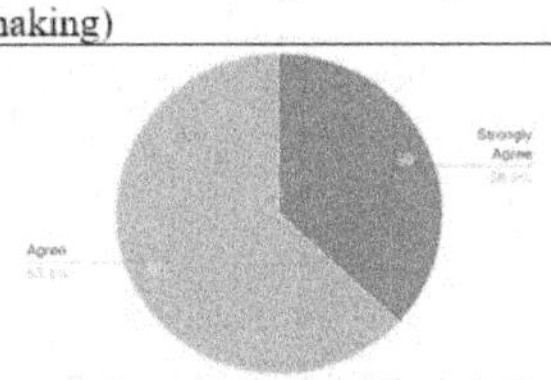

Inference: Agile leaders who opt for decentralized decision making, which entails transferring authority to where the relevant information is available, have earned overwhelming agreement from survey participants – an impressive 37% strongly agree and 63% simply agree.

Table 5. 20 Results of Survey Statement#11

Survey Statement#11: Agile leaders should proactively remove roadblocks at the organizational level

No.	Option	Frequency	Percentage
1	Strongly Agree	55	34.38%
2	Agree	105	65.63%
3	Neutral	0	0%
4	Disagree	0	0%
5	Strongly Disagree	0	0%
	Total	**160**	**100%**

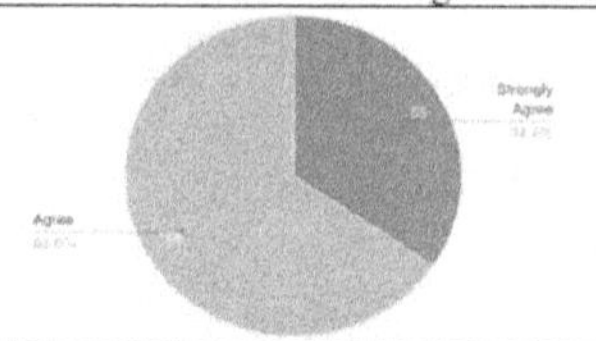

Inference: 34% of the respondents strongly agree and another 66% of the respondents agree that Agile leaders should proactively remove roadblocks at the organizational level. A clear majority of survey respondents demonstrated unequivocal support for Agile leaders taking the initiative to address organizational impediments.

Table 5. 21 Results of Survey Statement#12

Survey Statement#12: Training, coaching, mentoring provided by Agile coach on Agile methodologies and Agile mindset are essential for enterprise Agile transformation

No.	Option	Frequency	Percentage
1	Strongly Agree	68	42.50%
2	Agree	92	57.50%
3	Neutral	0	0%
4	Disagree	0	0%
5	Strongly Disagree	0	0%
	Total	**160**	**100%**

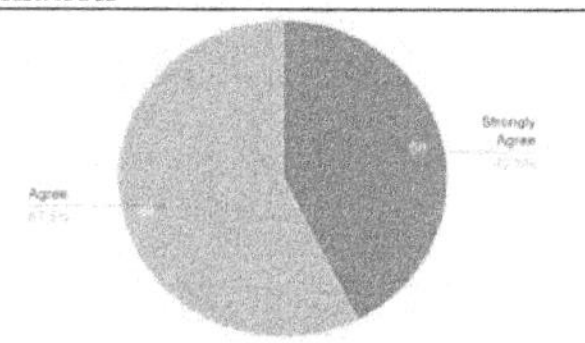

Inference: 100% of the respondents recognize that Training, coaching, and mentoring provided by an Agile coach on modern methodologies and mindsets are essential for enterprise agility. The vast majority feel strongly about this necessity in order to achieve successful transformations.

Table 5. 22 Results of Survey Statement#13

Survey Statement#13: Agile coaches must work closely with teams, executives, and business stakeholders to ensure the success of the Agile transformation

No.	Option	Frequency	Percentage
1	Strongly Agree	72	45.00%
2	Agree	88	55.00%
3	Neutral	0	0%
4	Disagree	0	0%
5	Strongly Disagree	0	0%
	Total	**160**	**100%**

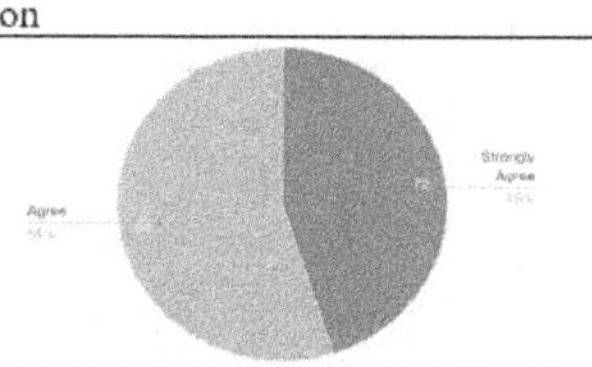

Inference: 45% of the respondents strongly agree and another 55% of the respondents agree that Agile coaches must work closely with teams, executives, and business stakeholders to ensure the success of the Agile transformation. Agile coaches are essential to foster success in Agile transformations, with an overwhelming majority of respondents emphasizing their importance. Working collaboratively and transparently with stakeholders across all organizational levels is necessary for a successful journey towards agility.

Table 5. 23 Results of Survey Statement#14

Survey Statement#14: Agile coaches must assess enterprise business agility on a regular basis and take appropriate actions to improve agility

No.	Option	Frequency	Percentage
1	Strongly Agree	80	50.00%
2	Agree	80	50.00%
3	Neutral	0	0%
4	Disagree	0	0%
5	Strongly Disagree	0	0%
	Total	**160**	**100%**

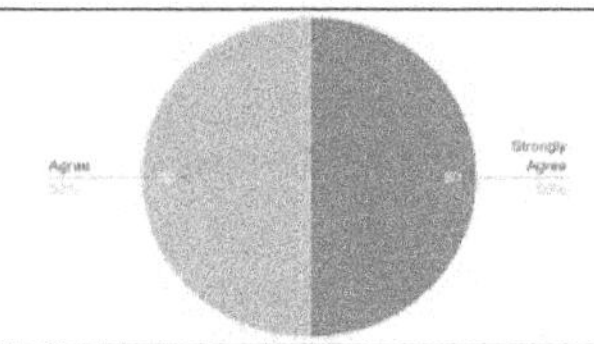

Inference: Agile coaches play a crucial role in assessing and improving enterprise business agility, with the majority of survey respondents being strongly supportive - 50% agreeing completely, and another 50% indicating their agreement. Keeping abreast on current issues is key to optimizing organizational readiness for growth.

Table 5. 24 Results of Survey Statement#15

Survey Statement#15: Agile coaches need to advocate suitable product engineering methods and help establish the governance model to support Agile approaches

No.	Option	Frequency	Percentage
1	Strongly Agree	66	41.25%
2	Agree	94	58.75%
3	Neutral	0	0%
4	Disagree	0	0%
5	Strongly Disagree	0	0%
	Total	**160**	**100%**

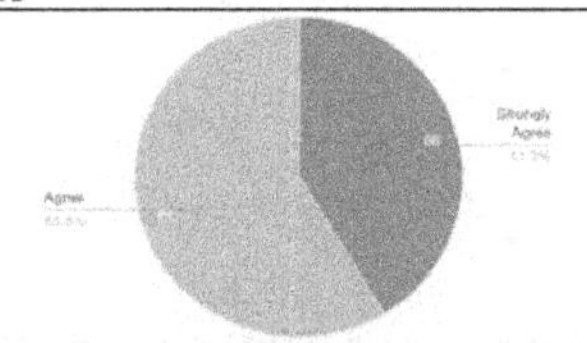

Inference: 41% of the respondents strongly agree and another 59% of the respondents agree that Agile coaches need to advocate suitable product engineering methods and help establish the governance model to support Agile approaches. The majority of respondents – a solid 100% - firmly believe that Agile coaches should take proactive steps to ensure the proper implementation of Agile approaches by championing suitable product engineering methods and instituting an effective governance model.

5.2.3. Survey Results for Hypothesis#3

Hypothesis#3: Sustaining as Agile enterprise is not important in digital era.

Table 5. 25 Results of Survey Statement#16

Survey Statement#16: To sustain as an Agile organization, relentless improvement should be part of the enterprise culture

No.	Option	Frequency	Percentage
1	Strongly Agree	67	41.88%
2	Agree	93	58.12%
3	Neutral	0	0%
4	Disagree	0	0%
5	Strongly Disagree	0	0%
	Total	**160**	**100%**

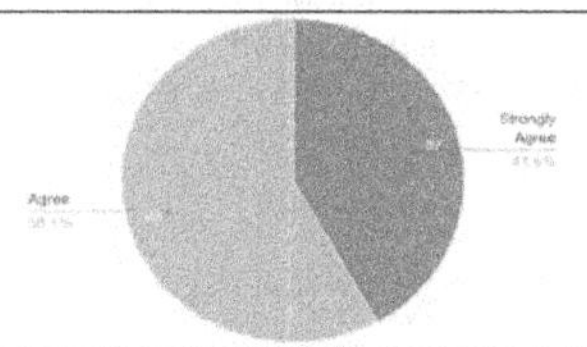

Inference: A remarkable majority of respondents agreed that to remain Agile and competitive, enterprises must continually strive for improvement - an impressive 42% strongly affirming the importance of this concept and another 58% of the respondents agreeing with it.

Table 5. 26 Results of Survey Statement#17

Survey Statement#17: To maintain agility, do you think organizational culture should encourage innovation without fear of negative consequences?

No.	Option	Frequency	Percentage
1	Strongly Agree	51	31.88%
2	Agree	109	68.12%
3	Neutral	0	0%
4	Disagree	0	0%
5	Strongly Disagree	0	0%
	Total	160	100%

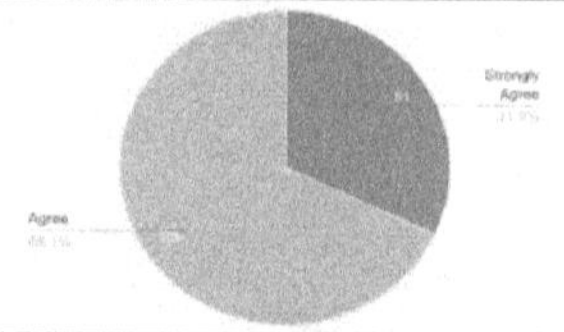

Inference: 32% of the respondents strongly agree and another 68% of the respondents agree that to maintain agility, organizational culture should encourage innovation without fear of negative consequences. Companies striving for agility should promote innovation without fear of repercussions.

Table 5. 27 Results of Survey Statement#18

Survey Statement#18: To remain an Agile enterprise, it is critical to share best practices throughout the enterprise (ex: via CoP-communities of practice)

No.	Option	Frequency	Percentage
1	Strongly Agree	47	29.38%
2	Agree	113	70.63%
3	Neutral	0	0%
4	Disagree	0	0%
5	Strongly Disagree	0	0%
	Total	160	100%

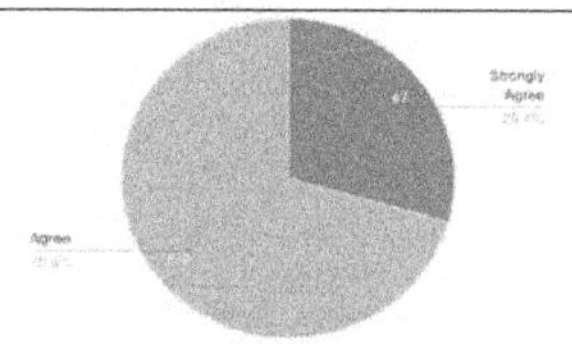

Inference: To remain Agile and competitive, it is essential that businesses foster an environment of knowledge sharing. The results demonstrate this mindset as nearly all respondents (100%) agree on the value in exchanging best practices throughout their organization.

Table 5. 28 Results of Survey Statement#19

Survey Statement#19: It is important for business teams to operate with Agile practices to sustain enterprise agility.

No.	Option	Frequency	Percentage
1	Strongly Agree	67	41.88%
2	Agree	93	58.12%
3	Neutral	0	0%
4	Disagree	0	0%
5	Strongly Disagree	0	0%
	Total	160	100%

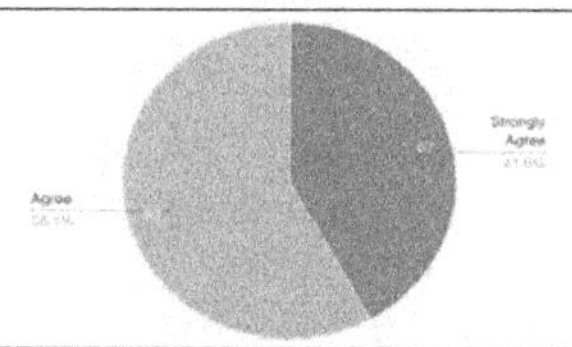

Inference: A solid majority of respondents have identified Agile practices as a critical element for driving and maintaining enterprise agility. A whopping 42% strongly agree, with 58% more in agreement - making it clear that this is an essential focus area for any business team looking to sustain success.

Table 5. 29 Results of Survey Statement#20

Survey Statement#20: Consistently sustaining as an Agile enterprise is a key in the digital era to compete in the market

No.	Option	Frequency	Percentage
1	Strongly Agree	61	38.13%
2	Agree	99	61.87%
3	Neutral	0	0%
4	Disagree	0	0%
5	Strongly Disagree	0	0%
Total		**160**	**100%**

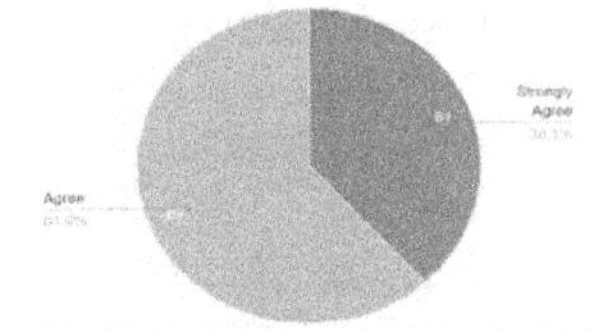

Inference: Companies of all sizes are increasingly recognizing the importance of staying nimble and Agile in order to navigate today's digital landscape effectively. An overwhelming majority expressed their agreement with this essential strategy for success.

Table 5. 30 Results of Survey Statement#21

Survey Statement#21: Understanding the fundamentals of the Agile mindset is crucial for all corporate personnel (across organizational boundaries) in order to sustain as an Agile enterprise

No.	Option	Frequency	Percentage
1	Strongly Agree	52	32.50%
2	Agree	107	66.88%
3	Neutral	1	0.63%
4	Disagree	0	0%
5	Strongly Disagree	0	0%
Total		**160**	**100%**

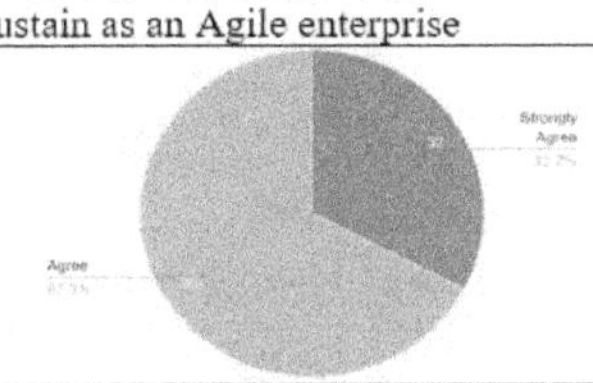

Inference: It is essential for companies to stay competitive in the long-term - and understanding the Agile mindset is key. Survey results demonstrate that an overwhelming majority of respondents (99%) recognize this, with 32% strongly agreeing and 67% simply agreeing. To ensure organizations remain Agile enterprises across all departments, comprehension of these fundamentals must be established throughout corporate personnel.

Table 5. 31 Results of Survey Statement#22

Survey Statement#22: The culture of creating a continuous learning supports enterprise agility

No.	Option	Frequency	Percentage
1	Strongly Agree	55	34.38%
2	Agree	105	65.62%
3	Neutral	0	0%
4	Disagree	0	0%
5	Strongly Disagree	0	0%
Total		**160**	**100%**

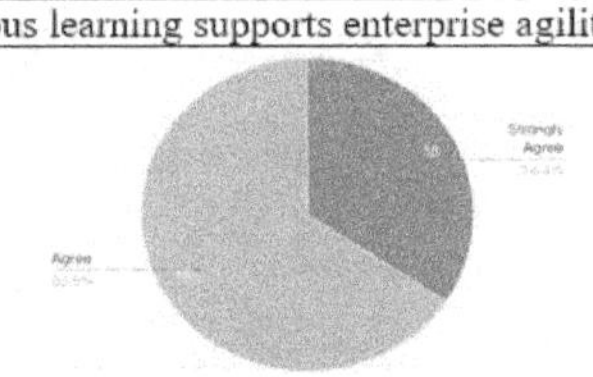

Inference: 34% of the respondents strongly agree and another 66% of the respondents agree that the culture of creating a continuous learning supports enterprise agility. Promoting a culture of learning can play an important role in helping enterprises become more Agile.

Table 5. 32 Results of Survey Statement#23

Survey Statement#23: In order to maintain enterprise agility, need not treat Agile as a strategic priority.

No.	Option	Frequency	Percentage
1	Strongly Agree	0	0%
2	Agree	0	0%
3	Neutral	0	0%
4	Disagree	67	41.88%
5	Strongly Disagree	93	58.13%
	Total	**160**	**100%**

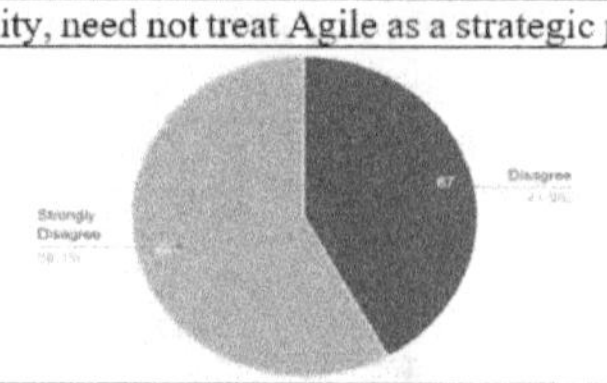

Inference: A staggering majority of respondents emphatically reject the notion that enterprise agility can be maintained without treating it as a strategic priority - with 42% disagreeing and an additional 58% strongly dissenting.

5.2.4. Survey Results for Hypothesis#4

Hypothesis#4: Agile methodologies are not key success factors for business & digital transformation.

Table 5. 33 Results of Survey Statement#24

Survey Statement#24: Agile scaling promotes digital transformation at the enterprise level

No.	Option	Frequency	Percentage
1	Strongly Agree	68	42.50%
2	Agree	92	57.50%
3	Neutral	0	0%
4	Disagree	0	0%
5	Strongly Disagree	0	0%
	Total	**160**	**100%**

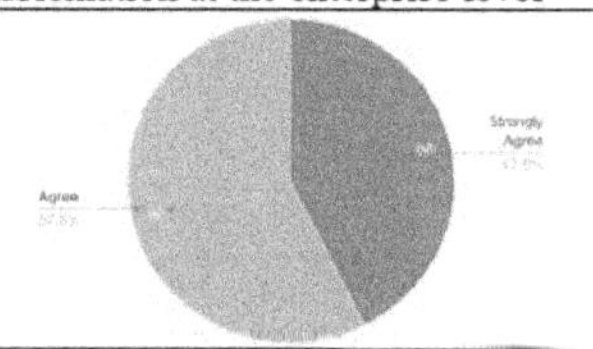

Inference: A staggering majority of survey respondents recognize that Agile scaling is a powerful tool in driving digital transformation at the enterprise level. 42% of the respondents strongly agree and another 58% of the respondents agree that Agile scaling promotes digital transformation at the enterprise level.

Table 5. 34 Results of Survey Statement#25

Survey Statement#25: Agile project management techniques do not support successful business and digital transformation

No.	Option	Frequency	Percentage
1	Strongly Agree	0	0%
2	Agree	0	0%
3	Neutral	0	0%
4	Disagree	70	43.75%
5	Strongly Disagree	90	56.25%
	Total	**160**	**100%**

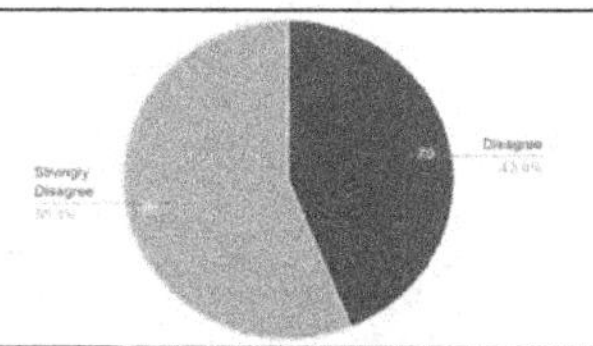

Inference: 44% of the respondents disagree and another 56% of the respondents strongly disagree that Agile project management techniques do not support successful business and digital transformation. This indicates strong opinion that Agile project management support successful business and digital transformation.

Table 5. 35 Results of Survey Statement#26

Survey Statement#26: The use of Agile methodologies in marketing activities is critical for business transformation

No.	Option	Frequency	Percentage
1	Strongly Agree	51	31.88%
2	Agree	109	68.13%
3	Neutral	0	0%
4	Disagree	0	0%
5	Strongly Disagree	0	0%
	Total	**160**	**100%**

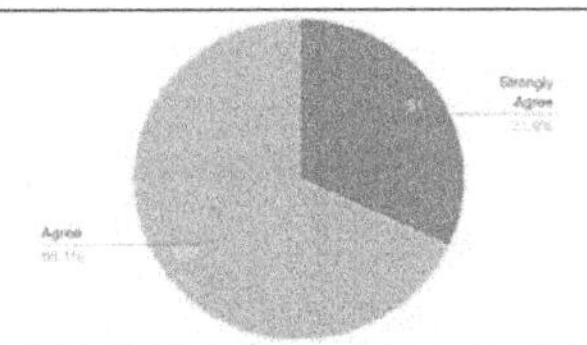

Inference: An overwhelming majority of respondents affirmed the importance of Agile methodologies in marketing activities, with a strong consensus that they are essential for successful business transformation. 32% of the respondents strongly agree and another 68% of the respondents agree that the use of Agile methodologies in marketing activities is critical for business transformation

Table 5. 36 Results of Survey Statement#27

Survey Statement#27: Applying Agile practices in HR functions is important for successful business and digital transformation

No.	Option	Frequency	Percentage
1	Strongly Agree	47	29.38%
2	Agree	113	70.63%
3	Neutral	0	0%
4	Disagree	0	0%
5	Strongly Disagree	0	0%
	Total	**160**	**100%**

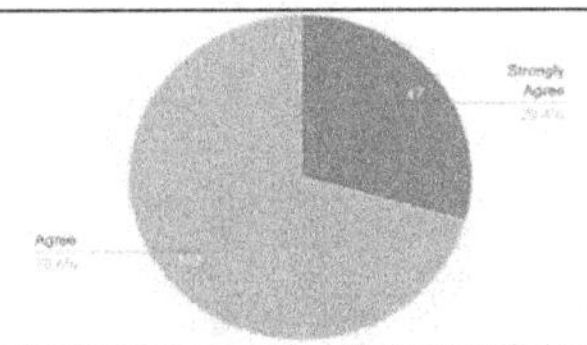

Inference: An overwhelming majority of respondents believe that Agile practices in HR functions are indispensable for achieving successful business and digital transformation outcomes. Specifically, 29% strongly agree with this notion while an additional 71% agree - emphasizing the integral role these approaches play in today's corporate environment.

Table 5. 37 Results of Survey Statement#28

Survey Statement#28: Adapting to best Agile practices increases the happiness index of employees

No.	Option	Frequency	Percentage
1	Strongly Agree	67	41.88%
2	Agree	93	58.13%
3	Neutral	0	0%
4	Disagree	0	0%
5	Strongly Disagree	0	0%
	Total	**160**	**100%**

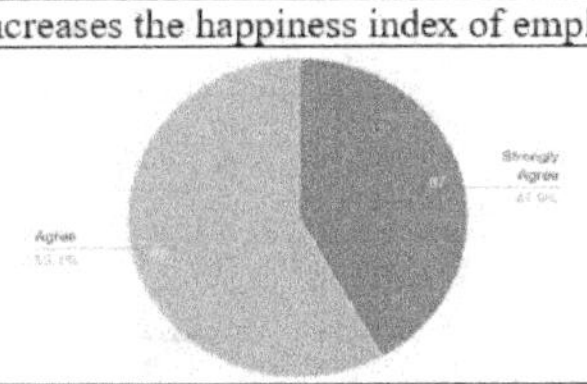

Inference: The survey results demonstrate that a majority of respondents recognize the power of Agile practices in fostering employee satisfaction – with an impressive 42% strongly agreeing, and 58% further confirming their agreement.

Table 5. 38 Results of Survey Statement#29

Survey Statement#29: Agile aids in the streamlining and improvement of business processes

No.	Option	Frequency	Percentage
1	Strongly Agree	61	38.13%
2	Agree	99	61.88%
3	Neutral	0	0%
4	Disagree	0	0%
5	Strongly Disagree	0	0%
	Total	**160**	**100%**

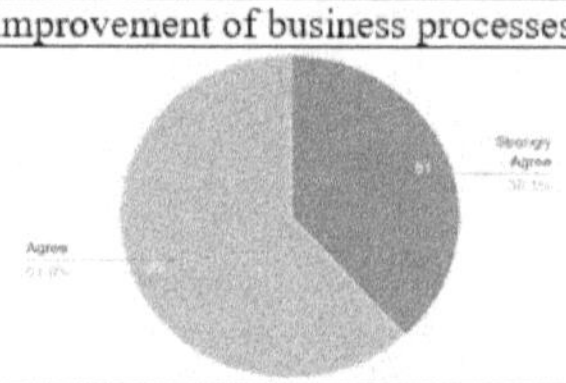

Inference: Agile is well-supported by the majority of respondents, with an overwhelming majority showing agreement that it helps streamline and improve business operations. 38% of the respondents strongly agree and another 62% of the respondents agree that Agile aids in the streamlining and improvement of business processes.

Table 5. 39 Results of Survey Statement#30

Survey Statement#30: Agile helps in the development of adaptable governance frameworks that can support business and digital transformation

No.	Option	Frequency	Percentage
1	Strongly Agree	70	43.75%
2	Agree	89	55.63%
3	Neutral	1	0.63%
4	Disagree	0	0%
5	Strongly Disagree	0	0%
	Total	**160**	**100%**

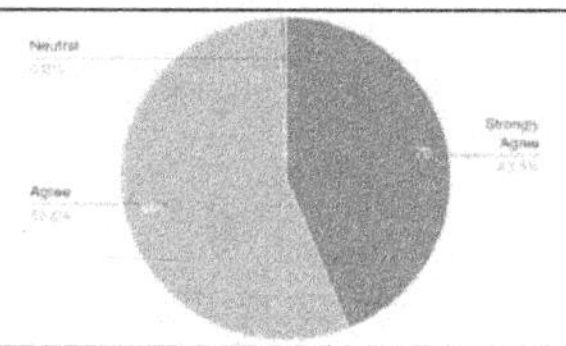

Inference: Agile is a powerful tool for helping organizations build resilient frameworks to ensure successful digital and business transformation. An overwhelming majority of respondents—an impressive 99% in total—either strongly agree or agree with this statement.

Table 5. 40 Results of Survey Statement#31

Survey Statement#31: Factors like Customer-centricity, design thinking, built-in quality, and an innovation mindset contribute to effective digital transformation

No.	Option	Frequency	Percentage
1	Strongly Agree	66	41.25%
2	Agree	94	58.75%
3	Neutral	0	0%
4	Disagree	0	0%
5	Strongly Disagree	0	0%
	Total	**160**	**100%**

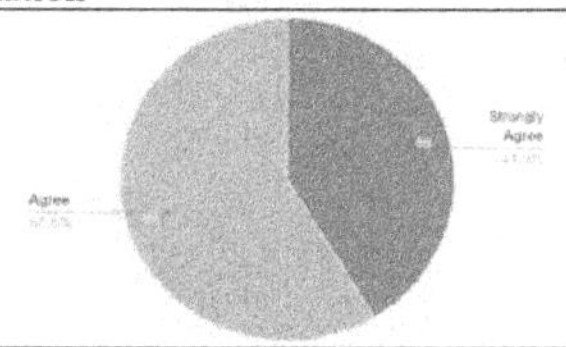

Inference: All the respondents acknowledged the importance of customer-centricity, design thinking and built-in quality in successful digital transformation journeys. Additionally, an innovation mindset was seen as a critical factor to ensure lasting success.

5.2.5. Survey Results for Hypothesis#5

Hypothesis#5: Agile adoption is not key to achieve enterprise business agility and overcome digital transformation challenges.

Table 5. 41 Results of Survey Statement#32

Survey Statement#32: Agile allows firms to better manage change and eliminate waste, which can help to reduce development costs

No.	Option	Frequency	Percentage
1	Strongly Agree	68	42.50%
2	Agree	92	57.50%
3	Neutral	0	0%
4	Disagree	0	0%
5	Strongly Disagree	0	0%
	Total	**160**	**100%**

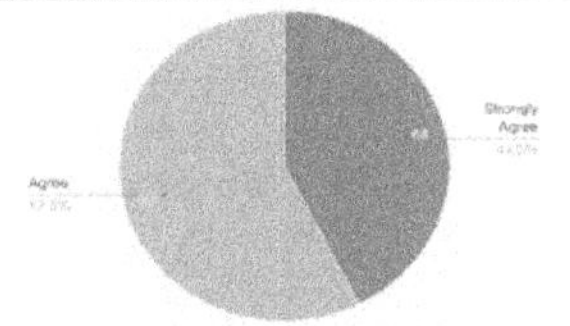

Inference: 42% of the respondents strongly agree and another 58% of the respondents agree that Agile allows firms to better manage change and eliminate waste, which can help to reduce development costs. Agile is a clear favorite among respondents, as an overwhelming majority of respondents see it as the solution to effectively managing change and reducing waste in order to lower development costs.

Table 5. 42 Results of Survey Statement#33

Survey Statement#33: Agile encourages greater teamwork and communication which can lead to successful results

No.	Option	Frequency	Percentage
1	Strongly Agree	57	35.63%
2	Agree	103	64.38%
3	Neutral	0	0%
4	Disagree	0	0%
5	Strongly Disagree	0	0%
	Total	**160**	**100%**

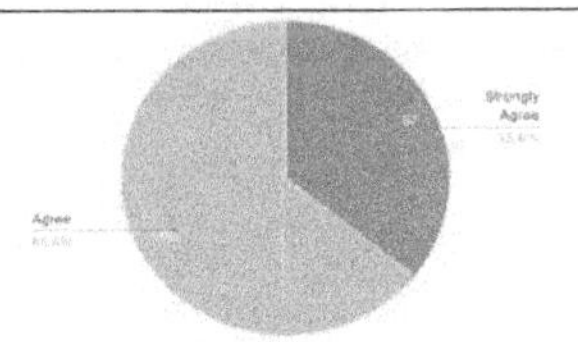

Inference: 36% of the respondents strongly agree and another 64% of the respondents agree that Agile encourages greater teamwork and communication which can lead to successful results. Respondents overwhelmingly believe that Agile methodology facilitates higher levels of collaboration and communication, which in turn can lead to highly successful outcomes.

Table 5. 43 Results of Survey Statement#34

Survey Statement#34: Agile does not assist IT businesses in delivering business value more quickly and efficiently

No.	Option	Frequency	Percentage
1	Strongly Agree	0	0%
2	Agree	0	0%
3	Neutral	0	0%
4	Disagree	55	34.38%
5	Strongly Disagree	105	65.63%
	Total	**160**	**100%**

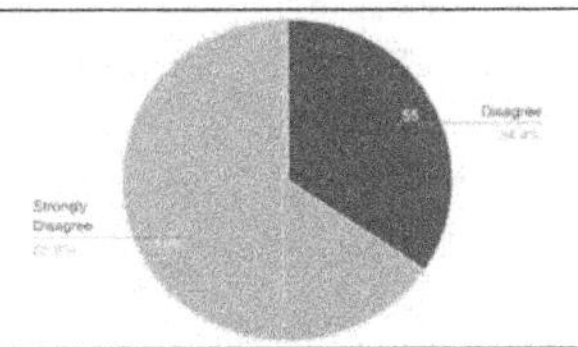

Inference: A majority of survey respondents strongly disagreed that Agile does not help IT businesses to realize business value more rapidly and effectively. 34% of the respondents disagree and another 66% of the respondents strongly disagree that Agile does not assist IT businesses in delivering business value more quickly and efficiently.

Table 5. 44 Results of Survey Statement#35

Survey Statement#35: Agile practices will help minimize the VUCA (volatile, uncertain, complex, ambiguous) challenges

No.	Option	Frequency	Percentage
1	Strongly Agree	75	46.88%
2	Agree	85	53.13%
3	Neutral	0	0%
4	Disagree	0	0%
5	Strongly Disagree	0	0%
	Total	**160**	**100%**

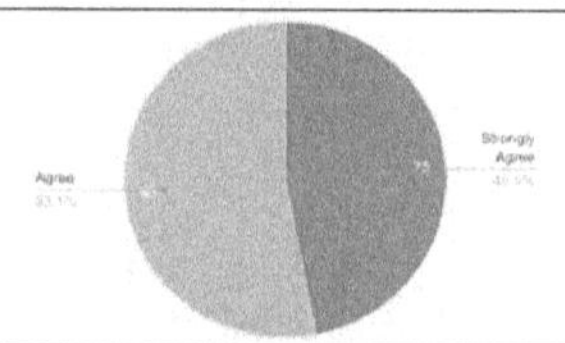

Inference: A majority of respondents are confident that Agile practices can offer effective solutions to combat the increasingly volatile, uncertain, complex and ambiguous (VUCA) business environment. A staggering 47% strongly agree with this notion while an additional 53% expressed agreement.

Table 5. 45 Results of Survey Statement#36

Survey Statement#36: Agile helps to foster a more open and collaborative culture in business organizations

No.	Option	Frequency	Percentage
1	Strongly Agree	64	40.00%
2	Agree	96	60.00%
3	Neutral	0	0%
4	Disagree	0	0%
5	Strongly Disagree	0	0%
	Total	**160**	**100%**

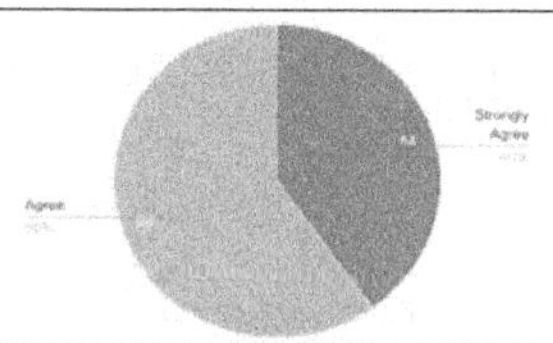

Inference: Agile have been widely embraced by business organizations for their positive impacts on fostering open and collaborative cultures; 40% expressing strong concurrence with this notion, while an additional 60% voicing agreement.

Table 5. 46 Results of Survey Statement#37

Survey Statement#37: Agile adoption aids in overcoming employee cross-cultural barriers, which promotes digital transformation

No.	Option	Frequency	Percentage
1	Strongly Agree	72	45.00%
2	Agree	84	52.50%
3	Neutral	4	2.50%
4	Disagree	0	0%
5	Strongly Disagree	0	0%
	Total	**160**	**100%**

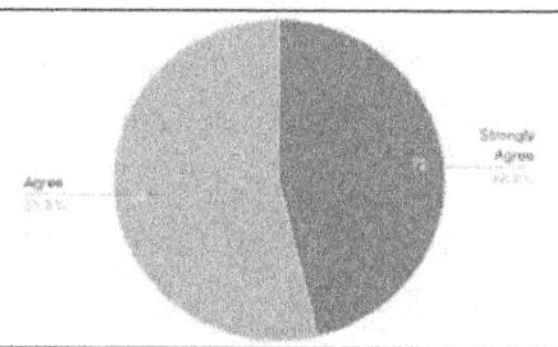

Inference: Adopting an Agile methodology is a key tool in unifying and driving successful digital transformation across cultures. An overwhelming majority of 97% reported satisfaction with the use of this approach to reduce cross-cultural tensions within their workforce.

Table 5. 47 Results of Survey Statement#38

Survey Statement#38: Agile practices such as Management 3.0, OKRs (Objectives and Key Results) help improve business agility

No.	Option	Frequency	Percentage
1	Strongly Agree	43	26.88%
2	Agree	112	70.00%
3	Neutral	5	3.13%
4	Disagree	0	0%
5	Strongly Disagree	0	0%
	Total	**160**	**100%**

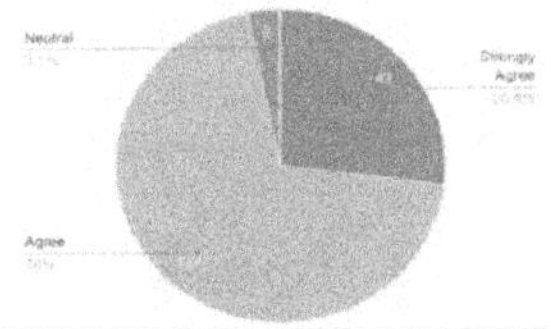

Inference: An overwhelming majority of survey respondents (97%) believe that Agile practices such as Management 3.0 and OKRs can bolster business agility, with 27% affirming their agreement in the strongest possible terms.

5.2.6. Survey Results for Generic Agile Questionnaire

Table 5. 48 Results of Survey Statement#39

Survey Statement#39: Most Practiced Agile Framework

No.	Option	Frequency	Percentage
1	Scrum	160	100.00%
2	Kanban	117	73.10%
3	Scrumban	85	53.10%
4	Lean	93	58.10%
5	DevOps or DevSecOps	116	72.50%
6	SAFe (Scaled Agile Framework)	147	91.90%
7	LeSS	51	31.90%
8	Xtreme Programming (XP)	84	52.50%
9	Feature Driven Development (FDD)	44	27.50%
10	Test Driven Development (TDD)	73	45.60%
11	ScrumofScrums	127	79.40%
12	Scrum@Scale	75	46.90%
13	Disciplined Agile Delivery (DAD)	17	10.60%
14	Dynamic Systems Development Method (DSDM)	20	12.50%
15	AgileSHIFT framework	34	21.30%
16	Hybrid Framework	72	45.00%

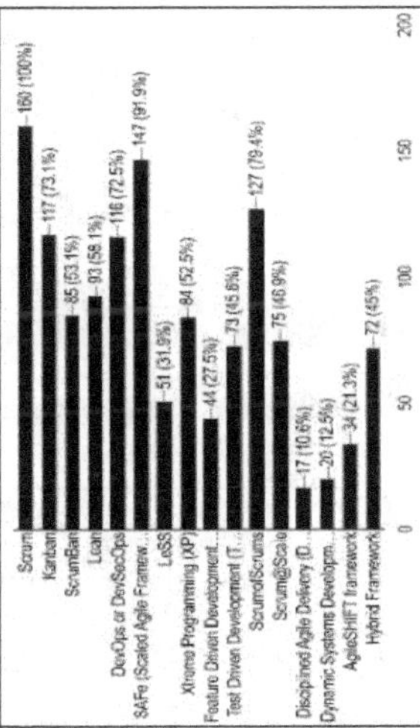

Inference: Scrum is the most practiced (100%) Agile Framework by all the respondents of the survey, followed by Scaled Agile (91.9%), Kanban and DevOps or DevSecOps (73 & 72%% each), Lean (58%) and Scrumban (53%). Other frameworks practiced by the respondents include Hybrid (45%), LeSS (31.9%).

Table 5. 49 Results of Survey Statement#40

Survey Statement#40: What are the main reasons for companies to adopt Agile practices?

No.	Option	Frequency	Percentage
1	Business/IT Alignment	141	88.10%
2	Productivity Increase	154	96.30%
3	Better Quality	157	98.10%
4	Ease of Managing product delivery	135	84.40%
5	Faster time to market	143	89.40%
6	Regular feedback cycle increases value creation	158	98.80%
7	Ease of managing HR hiring process	76	47.50%
8	Ease of managing Marketing activities	59	36.9%
9	Ease of managing distributed Teams	4	2.5%
10	Predictability	4	2.5%
11	Project transparency	3	1.9%
12	Risk Reduction	3	1.9%
13	Increase predictability	2	1.3%
14	Better portfolio level alignment	1	0.6%
15	Ease of portfolio level organization	1	0.6%
16	To adapt changing market needs	1	0.6%
17	Better alignment between multiple teams	1	0.6%
18	Portfolio level alignment	1	0.6%
19	One enterprise with one working culture	1	0.6%
20	Transparency of the project	1	0.6%
21	Manage Priorities	1	0.6%
22	Easy to manage changing priorities	1	0.6%
23	Predictability	1	0.6%
24	Reduction Risk	1	0.6%
25	Easy Governance	1	0.6%
26	Increase project transparency	1	0.6%
27	Increase transparency	1	0.6%
28	Ease of managing of predictability	1	0.6%
29	Reduction of Risk	1	0.6%
30	Ease of managing distributed teams	1	0.6%
31	Increase predictability	1	0.6%

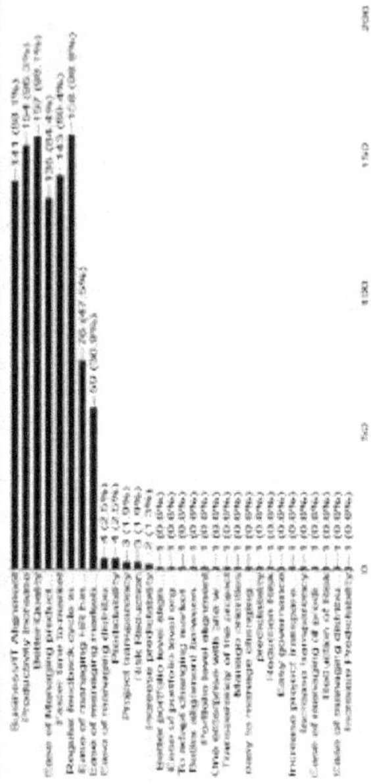

Inference: Agile practices offer a host of advantages for companies, such as improved quality standards and productivity gains. These can lead to immense value creation opportunities alongside faster routes to market - all the while ensuring successful alignment between business functions and IT teams. Additionally, Agile solutions facilitate smoother product delivery processes coupled with streamlined HR & marketing operations.

Table 5. 50 Results of Survey Statement#41

Survey Statement#41: What was the most difficult challenge your organization faced during an Agile transformation?

No.	Option	Frequency	Percentage
1	Absence of Agile Coach	136	85.00%
2	Inconsistent Processes	129	80.60%
3	Resistant to change	130	81.30%
4	Insufficient Training	148	92.50%
5	Lack of Experience	141	88.10%
6	Organisational Culture	142	88.20%
7	Inefficient Leadership	124	77.50%
8	Lack of collaboration	144	90.00%
9	Lack of understanding of Agile methods	133	83.10%
10	Implementation failures due to inadequate planning	106	66.30%
11	Inadequate resources or support from upper management	132	82.50%
12	Unrealistic expectations about the outcomes of the transition	53	33.10%
13	Business teams not operating in Agile	1	0.6%
14	Hurry in transformation	1	0.6%

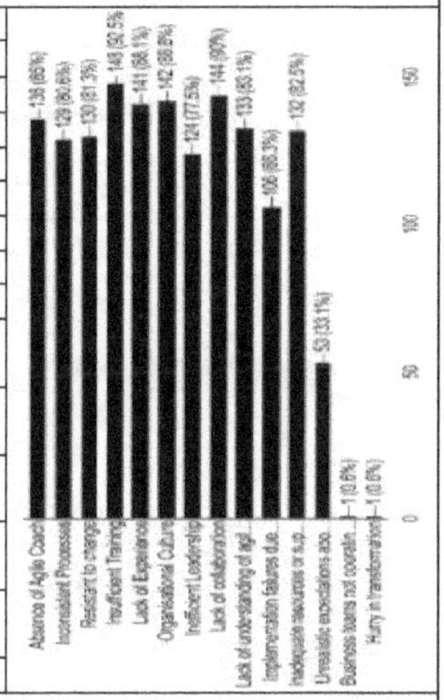

Inference: Organizations face different challenges (as shown in the table) during an Agile transformation. Top voted challenges are: insufficient training (92.5%), lack of collaboration (90%), organization culture (88.8%) and absence of Agile coach (85%). To overcome these challenges, require a better solution approach backed with expertise and understanding of the methods, so that Agile implementation will be successful.

5.3 Interpretation of Survey Results

5.3.1 Reliability Measure

The stability or consistency of test results is measured by reliability. It can also be viewed as the capability of a test or a set of research findings to be replicated. How well your test truly measures what you want it to assess is determined by its internal consistency. How accurately a test evaluates achievement is determined by its reliability coefficient. It is the percentage of the variation in observed scores—that is, test scores—that may be attributed to real scores. The most popular internal consistency coefficient is Cronbach's alpha. Cronbach's alpha tests are used to determine the reliability of surveys with several Likert scale questions. These inquiries gauge hidden or unobservable factors called latent variables, such as a person's conscientiousness, neurosis, or openness. In the actual world, these are incredibly challenging to quantify. How closely connected a group of test items are to one another can be determined by Cronbach's alpha.

The following is a general guide for interpreting the findings (Cronbach, 1951).

Table 5. 51 Rule of Thumb for Reliability Measure (Cronbach's Alpha)

Cronbach's Alpha	Internal Consistency
$\alpha \geq 0.9$	Excellent
$0.8 \leq \alpha < 0.9$	Good
$0.7 \leq \alpha < 0.8$	Acceptable
$0.6 \leq \alpha < 0.7$	Questionable
$0.5 \leq \alpha < 0.6$	Poor
$\alpha < 0.5$	Unacceptable

Source: Cronbach (1951)

Reliability test result for variable selected to evaluate importance of Agile dimensions in IT sector are shown below.

Table 5. 52 Reliability Measure Results

Scale: ALL VARIABLES

Case Processing Summary

		N	%
Cases	Valid	160	100.0
	Excluded[a]	0	.0
	Total	160	100.0

a. Listwise deletion based on all variables in the procedure.

Reliability Statistics

Cronbach's Alpha	N of Items
.915	33

Statistics for Cronbach's Alpha reliability are shown in the results table above. 75% of variables (33 variables) were used as input and SPSS 29.0 version was used for analysis. The output result was 0.915. According to the general guideline for evaluating result values, the measuring variables and study scores are **Excellent**.

5.3.2 Mean, Standard Deviation, Variance and Inferences

In this sub chapter, we will discuss about the importance of Mean, Standard Deviation and Variances Statistical analysis for the study.

5.3.2.1. Mean

The most popular way to find averages is to use the mean, usually referred to as "M."

Sample Mean

$$\bar{X} = \frac{\sum x}{n} = \frac{\text{Sum of All the Items in Sample}}{\text{(Number of Items in Sample - 1)}}$$

As shown in the above formula, by adding up the values of each response and dividing the total by the "N" number of responses, you may determine the mean. The sample mean is helpful because it enables you to make estimates about the behavior of the entire population without having to poll everyone (University of Barotseland, 2014).

5.3.2.2. Standard Deviation

Dataset's average level of variability is represented by the standard deviation (s), which displays the variance of each score in relation to the mean. Your dataset's variable will be more significant the higher your standard deviation. In statistics, the standard deviation serves as a measure of dispersion. Data's "dispersement" shows how widely dispersed it is. It specifically displays the degree to which your data are dispersed around the mean or average (Streiner, David L, 1996).

$$\sigma = \sqrt{\frac{\sum f \cdot (x_i - \mu)^2}{\sum f}}$$

- μ is the mean for the frequency distribution,
- f is the individual frequency counts,
- x is the value associated with the frequencies.

Above is the formula to find the standard deviation for a frequency distribution.

5.3.2.3. Variance

The spread of the dataset is reflected in the variance. The variation in relation to the mean increases with the degree of data spread. By simply squaring the standard deviation, we can obtain the variance. A CV >= 1 generally denotes a rather high variance, whereas a CV < 1 can be regarded as low (Kleinbaum DG, Kupper LL, Muller KE, 1988).

σ2M = σ2 / N σ^2_M = variance of the sampling distribution of the sample mean.
σ^2 = population variance.
N = sample size.

Above is the formula to find the variance of the sampling distribution of the mean.

5.3.2.4. Data Analysis Table with Mean, Standard Deviation, Variance

Table 5. 53 Mean. Standard Deviation and Variance Results

Variable Code	Survey Statement	N	Mean	Result Inference	Std. Deviation	Result Inference	Variance	Result Inference
Challenge1	Agile transformation in an organization is influenced by the support of its leadership team	160	4.563	Strongly Agree	.496	Low Deviation	.246	Low Variance
Challenge2	Inter-team communication plays no role in an organization's Agile transformation	160	4.437	Strongly Disagree	.496	Low Deviation	.246	Low Variance
Challenge3	Failure to invest in talent impedes the successful transformation of Agile	160	4.425	Strongly Agree	.494	Low Deviation	.244	Low Variance
Challenge4	Unclear organizational structure (roles and responsibilities) hinders Agile transformation	160	4.356	Strongly Agree	.479	Low Deviation	.229	Low Variance

Challenge5	Right tools are essential for a successful Agile transformation	160	4.294	Strongly Agree	.469	High Deviation	.220	Low Variance
Challenge6	Employee's resistance to culture shift can be a challenge in Agile transformation	160	4.525	Strongly Agree	.499	Low Deviation	.249	Low Variance
Challenge7	Agile transformation is not hampered by improperly applying Agile techniques	160	4.538	Strongly Disagree	.499	Low Deviation	.249	Low Variance
LeaderCoach1	Agile Leadership should clearly communicate the compelling change vision and exhibit openness to an Agile way of working	160	4.500	Strongly Agree	.500	Low Deviation	.250	Low Variance
LeaderCoach2	Agile leaders do not have to lead by example and authenticity	160	4.581	Strongly Disagree	.493	Low Deviation	.243	Low Variance
LeaderCoach3	Agile leaders should transfer the decision-making authority to where the information is available (known as decentralized decision making)	160	4.369	Strongly Agree	.482	Low Deviation	.233	Low Variance
LeaderCoach4	Agile leaders should proactively remove roadblocks at the organizational level	160	4.344	Strongly Agree	.475	Low Deviation	.226	Low Variance
LeaderCoach5	Training, coaching, mentoring provided by Agile coach on Agile methodologies and Agile mindset are essential for enterprise Agile transformation	160	4.425	Strongly Agree	.494	Low Deviation	.244	Low Variance
LeaderCoach6	Agile coaches must work closely with teams, executives, and business stakeholders to ensure the success of the Agile transformation	160	4.450	Strongly Agree	.497	Low Deviation	.248	Low Variance

LeaderCoach7	Agile coaches must assess enterprise business agility on a regular basis and take appropriate actions to improve agility	160	4.500	Strongly Agree	.500	Low Deviation	.250	Low Variance
LeaderCoach8	Agile coaches need to advocate suitable product engineering methods and help establish the governance model to support Agile approaches	160	4.413	Strongly Agree	.492	Low Deviation	.242	Low Variance
SustainAgile1	To sustain as an Agile organization, relentless improvement should be part of the enterprise culture	160	4.419	Strongly Agree	.493	Low Deviation	.243	Low Variance
SustainAgile2	To maintain agility, do you think organizational culture should encourage innovation without fear of negative consequences?	160	4.319	Strongly Agree	.466	Low Deviation	.217	Low Variance
SustainAgile3	To remain an Agile enterprise, it is critical to share best practices throughout the enterprise (ex: via CoP-communities of practice)	160	4.294	Strongly Agree	.455	Low Deviation	.207	Low Variance
SustainAgile4	It is important for business teams to operate with Agile practices to sustain enterprise agility	160	4.419	Strongly Agree	.493	Low Deviation	.243	Low Variance
SustainAgile5	Consistently sustaining as an Agile enterprise is a key in the digital era to compete in the market	160	4.381	Strongly Agree	.486	Low Deviation	.236	Low Variance

SustainAgile6	Understanding the fundamentals of the Agile mindset is crucial for all corporate personnel (across organizational boundaries) in order to sustain as an Agile enterprise	160	4.319	Strongly Agree	.479	High Deviation	.230	Low Variance
SustainAgile7	The culture of creating a continuous learning supports enterprise agility	160	4.344	Strongly Agree	.475	Low Deviation	.226	Low Variance
SustainAgile8	In order to maintain enterprise agility, need not treat Agile as a strategic priority	160	4.581	Strongly Disagree	.493	Low Deviation	.243	Low Variance
BDTransformation1	Agile scaling promotes digital transformation at the enterprise level	160	4.425	Strongly Agree	.494	Low Deviation	.244	Low Variance
BDTransformation2	Agile project management techniques do not support successful business and digital transformation	160	4.562	Strongly Disagree	.496	Low Deviation	.246	Low Variance
BDTransformation3	The use of Agile methodologies in marketing activities is critical for business transformation	160	4.319	Strongly Agree	.466	Low Deviation	.217	Low Variance
BDTransformation4	Applying Agile practices in HR functions is important for successful business and digital transformation	160	4.294	Strongly Agree	.455	Low Deviation	.207	Low Variance
BDTransformation5	Adapting to best Agile practices increases the happiness index of employees	160	4.419	Strongly Agree	.493	Low Deviation	.243	Low Variance
BDTransformation6	Agile aids in the streamlining and improvement of business processes	160	4.381	Strongly Agree	.486	Low Deviation	.236	Low Variance
BDTransformation7	Agile helps in the development of adaptable governance frameworks that can support business and	160	4.431	Strongly Agree	.508	High Deviation	.258	Low Variance

	digital transformation							
BDTransformations8	Factors like Customer-centricity, design thinking, built-in quality, and an innovation mindset contribute to effective digital transformation	160	4.412	Strongly Agree	.492	Low Deviation	.242	Low Variance
BusinessAgility 1	Agile allows firms to better manage change and eliminate waste, which can help to reduce development costs	160	4.425	Strongly Agree	.494	Low Deviation	.244	Low Variance
BusinessAgility 2	Agile encourages greater teamwork and communication which can lead to successful results	160	4.356	Strongly Agree	.479	Low Deviation	.229	Low Variance
BusinessAgility 3	Agile does not assist IT businesses in delivering business value more quickly and efficiently	160	4.656	Strongly Disagree	.475	Low Deviation	.226	Low Variance
BusinessAgility 4	Agile practices will help minimize the VUCA (volatile, uncertain, complex, ambiguous) challenges	160	4.469	Strongly Agree	.499	Low Deviation	.249	Low Variance
BusinessAgility 5	Agile helps to foster a more open and collaborative culture in business organizations	160	4.400	Strongly Agree	.490	Low Deviation	.240	Low Variance
BusinessAgility 6	Agile adoption aids in overcoming employee cross-cultural barriers, which promotes digital transformation	160	4.425	Strongly Agree	.543	High Deviation	.294	Low Variance
BusinessAgility 7	Agile practices such as Management 3.0, OKRs (Objectives and Key Results) help improve business agility	160	4.238	Strongly Agree	.494	High Deviation	.244	Low Variance
Valid N (listwise)		160						

With the calculation of mean, standard deviation and variance values, it is inferred that there no values to be standardized since the average responses for each survey questionnaire is either "Strongly Agree" or "Strongly Disagree.

5.3.3 Correlations

How to measure the linear relationship between two variables (quantitative)? A correlation (Pearson correlation) is used, value range is -1 to +1.

Table 5. 54 Rule of Thumb for Correlation Interpretation

Size of Correlation	Interpretation
.90 to 1.00 (−.90 to −1.00)	Very high positive (negative) correlation
.70 to .90 (−.70 to −.90)	High positive (negative) correlation
.50 to .70 (−.50 to −.70)	Moderate positive (negative) correlation
.30 to .50 (−.30 to −.50)	Low positive (negative) correlation
.00 to .30 (.00 to −.30)	negligible correlation

Source: Schober, Boer, & Schwarte. (2018)

As shown in the above table, higher scores on one measure imply lower scores on the other when the correlation is greater than 1, indicating a complete linear descending association. A correlation of 0 denotes the complete absence of any linear relationship between the two variables. Nevertheless, there might still be a (strong) non-linear relationship. Greater scores on one measure correlate with higher ratings on the other variable when the correlation is 1, signifying a perfect ascending linear relationship (Schober, Boer, & Schwarte, 2018).

5.3.3.1. Correlation Analysis for Hypothesis#1

Hypothesis#1: Overcoming Agile adoption challenges is not important to implement Agile and transform as an Agile Enterprise.

Below tables shows the correlation between variables of the hypothesis#1.

Table 5. 55 Correlation for Hypothesis#1

Correlations								
		Challenge1	Challenge2	Challenge3	Challenge4	Challenge5	Challenge6	Challenge7
Challenge1	Pearson Correlation	1	.448**	.299**	.209**	.149	.221**	.395**
	Sig. (2-tailed)		<,001	<,001	.008	.059	.005	<,001
	N	160	160	160	160	160	160	160
Challenge2	Pearson Correlation	.448**	1	.185*	.107	.119	.158*	.414**
	Sig. (2-tailed)	<,001		.019	.179	.133	.046	<,001
	N	160	160	160	160	160	160	160
Challenge3	Pearson Correlation	.299**	.185*	1	.522**	.243**	.160*	.189*
	Sig. (2-tailed)	<,001	.019		<,001	.002	.044	.017
	N	160	160	160	160	160	160	160
Challenge4	Pearson Correlation	.209**	.107	.522**	1	.285**	.237**	.167*
	Sig. (2-tailed)	.008	.179	<,001		<,001	.003	.035
	N	160	160	160	160	160	160	160
Challenge5	Pearson Correlation	.149	.119	.243**	.285**	1	.195*	.287**
	Sig. (2-tailed)	.059	.133	.002	<,001		.013	<,001
	N	160	160	160	160	160	160	160
Challenge6	Pearson Correlation	.221**	.158*	.160*	.237**	.195*	1	.297**
	Sig. (2-tailed)	.005	.046	.044	.003	.013		<,001
	N	160	160	160	160	160	160	160
Challenge7	Pearson Correlation	.395**	.414**	.189*	.167*	.287**	.297**	1
	Sig. (2-tailed)	<,001	<,001	.017	.035	<,001	<,001	
	N	160	160	160	160	160	160	160
**. Correlation is significant at the 0.01 level (2-tailed).								
*. Correlation is significant at the 0.05 level (2-tailed).								

From the above green highlighted table values, following are inferred.

0.448 infers that there is a low positive opinion relationship among "Agile transformation in an organization is influenced by the support of its leadership team" and "Inter-team communication plays NO role in an organization's Agile transformation".

0.299 infers that there is a negligible opinion relationship among "Agile transformation in an organization is influenced by the support of its leadership team" and "Failure to invest in talent impedes the successful transformation of Agile".

0.209 infers that there is a negligible opinion relationship among "Agile transformation in an organization is influenced by the support of its leadership team" and "Unclear organizational structure (roles and responsibilities) hinders Agile transformation".

0.149 infers that there is a negligible opinion relationship among "Agile transformation in an organization is influenced by the support of its leadership team" and "Right tools are essential for a successful Agile transformation".

0.221 infers that there is a negligible opinion relationship among "Agile transformation in an organization is influenced by the support of its leadership team" and "Employee's resistance to culture shift can be a challenge in Agile transformation".

0.395 infers that there is a low positive opinion relationship among "Agile transformation in an organization is influenced by the support of its leadership team" and "Agile transformation is NOT hampered by improperly applying Agile techniques".

0.522 infers that there is a moderate positive opinion relationship among "Failure to invest in talent impedes the successful transformation of Agile" and "Unclear organizational structure (roles and responsibilities) hinders Agile transformation".

Similarly, among other variables, it is inferred that there is negligible and low positive opinion relationship exists.

5.3.3.2. Correlation Analysis for Hypothesis#2

Hypothesis 2: Agile Leadership and Agile Coaching are not critical success factors in adopting Agile & transformation in IT Companies.

Below tables shows the correlation between variables of the hypothesis#2.

Table 5. 56 Correlation for Hypothesis#2

Correlations									
		Leader Coach 1	Leader Coach 2	Leader Coach 3	Leader Coach 4	Leader Coach 5	Leader Coach 6	Leader Coach 7	Leader Coach 8
Leader Coach 1	Pearson Correlation	1	.241**	.272**	.197*	.253**	.276**	.100	.254**
	Sig. (2-tailed)		.002	<,001	.012	.001	<,001	.208	.001
	N	160	160	160	160	160	160	160	160
Leader Coach 2	Pearson Correlation	.241**	1	.097	.108	.166*	.233**	.190*	.197*
	Sig. (2-tailed)	.002		.221	.176	.036	.003	.016	.013
	N	160	160	160	160	160	160	160	160
Leader Coach 3	Pearson Correlation	.272**	.097	1	.565**	.260**	.324**	.246**	.175*
	Sig. (2-tailed)	<,001	.221		<,001	<,001	<,001	.002	.027
	N	160	160	160	160	160	160	160	160
Leader Coach 4	Pearson Correlation	.197*	.108	.565**	1	.443**	.165*	.303**	.222**
	Sig. (2-tailed)	.012	.176	<,001		<,001	.037	<,001	.005
	N	160	160	160	160	160	160	160	160
Leader Coach 5	Pearson Correlation	.253**	.166*	.260**	.443**	1	.366**	.303**	.358**
	Sig. (2-tailed)	.001	.036	<,001	<,001		<,001	<,001	<,001
	N	160	160	160	160	160	160	160	160
Leader Coach 6	Pearson Correlation	.276**	.233**	.324**	.165*	.366**	1	.377**	.288**
	Sig. (2-tailed)	<,001	.003	<,001	.037	<,001		<,001	<,001
	N	160	160	160	160	160	160	160	160
Leader Coach 7	Pearson Correlation	.100	.190*	.246**	.303**	.303**	.377**	1	.330**
	Sig. (2-tailed)	.208	.016	.002	<,001	<,001	<,001		<,001
	N	160	160	160	160	160	160	160	160
Leader Coach 8	Pearson Correlation	.254**	.197*	.175*	.222**	.358**	.288**	.330**	1
	Sig. (2-tailed)	.001	.013	.027	.005	<,001	<,001	<,001	
	N	160	160	160	160	160	160	160	160
**. Correlation is significant at the 0.01 level (2-tailed).									
*. Correlation is significant at the 0.05 level (2-tailed).									

From the above green highlighted table values, following are inferred.

0.241 infers that there is a negligible opinion relationship among "Agile Leadership should clearly communicate the compelling change vision and exhibit openness to an Agile way of working" and "Agile leaders do NOT have to lead by example and authenticity".

0.272 infers that there is a negligible opinion relationship among "Agile Leadership should clearly communicate the compelling change vision and exhibit openness to an Agile way of working" and "Agile leaders should transfer the decision-making authority to where the information is available (known as decentralized decision making)".

0.197 infers that there is a negligible opinion relationship among "Agile Leadership should clearly communicate the compelling change vision and exhibit openness to an Agile way of working" and "Agile leaders should proactively remove roadblocks at the organizational level".

0.253 infers that there is a negligible opinion relationship among "Agile Leadership should clearly communicate the compelling change vision and exhibit openness to an Agile way of working" and "Training, coaching, mentoring provided by Agile coach on Agile methodologies and Agile mindset are essential for enterprise Agile transformation".

0.276 infers that there is a negligible opinion relationship among "Agile Leadership should clearly communicate the compelling change vision and exhibit openness to an Agile way of working" and "Agile coaches must work closely with teams, executives, and business stakeholders to ensure the success of the Agile transformation".

0.100 infers that there is a negligible opinion relationship among "Agile Leadership should clearly communicate the compelling change vision and exhibit openness to an Agile way of working" and "Agile coaches must assess enterprise business agility on a regular basis and take appropriate actions to improve agility".

0.254 infers that there is a negligible opinion relationship among "Agile Leadership should clearly communicate the compelling change vision and exhibit openness to an Agile way of working" and "Agile coaches need to advocate suitable product engineering methods and help establish the governance model to support Agile approaches".

0.565 infers that there is a moderate positive opinion relationship among "Agile leaders should transfer the decision-making authority to where the information is available (known as decentralized decision making)" and "Agile leaders should proactively remove roadblocks at the organizational level".

Similarly, among other variables, it is inferred that there is negligible and low positive opinion relationship exists.

5.3.3.3. Correlation Analysis for Hypothesis#3

Hypothesis 3: Sustaining as Agile enterprise is not important in digital era.
Below tables shows the correlation between variables of the hypothesis#3.

Table 5. 57 Correlation for Hypothesis#3

Correlations									
		SustainAgile1	SustainAgile2	SustainAgile3	SustainAgile4	SustainAgile5	SustainAgile6	SustainAgile7	SustainAgile8
SustainAgile1	Pearson Correlation	1	.534**	.398**	.230**	.273**	.255**	.293**	.361**
	Sig. (2-tailed)		<,001	<,001	.003	<,001	.001	<,001	<,001
	N	160	160	160	160	160	160	160	160
SustainAgile2	Pearson Correlation	.534**	1	.472**	.208**	.402**	.245**	.296**	.227**
	Sig. (2-tailed)	<,001		<,001	.008	<,001	.002	<,001	.004
	N	160	160	160	160	160	160	160	160
SustainAgile3	Pearson Correlation	.398**	.472**	1	.398**	.200*	.258**	.342**	.241**
	Sig. (2-tailed)	<,001	<,001		<,001	.011	<,001	<,001	.002
	N	160	160	160	160	160	160	160	160
SustainAgile4	Pearson Correlation	.230**	.208**	.398**	1	.299**	.202*	.293**	.207**
	Sig. (2-tailed)	.003	.008	<,001		<,001	.010	<,001	.009
	N	160	160	160	160	160	160	160	160
SustainAgile5	Pearson Correlation	.273**	.402**	.200*	.299**	1	.230**	.163*	.327**
	Sig. (2-tailed)	<,001	<,001	.011	<,001		.003	.039	<,001
	N	160	160	160	160	160	160	160	160
SustainAgile6	Pearson Correlation	.255**	.245**	.258**	.202*	.230**	1	.315**	.327**
	Sig. (2-tailed)	.001	.002	<,001	.010	.003		<,001	<,001
	N	160	160	160	160	160	160	160	160
SustainAgile7	Pearson Correlation	.293**	.296**	.342**	.293**	.163*	.315**	1	.214**
	Sig. (2-tailed)	<,001	<,001	<,001	<,001	.039	<,001		.007
	N	160	160	160	160	160	160	160	160
SustainAgile8	Pearson Correlation	.361**	.227**	.241**	.207**	.327**	.327**	.214**	1
	Sig. (2-tailed)	<,001	.004	.002	.009	<,001	<,001	.007	
	N	160	160	160	160	160	160	160	160
**. Correlation is significant at the 0.01 level (2-tailed).									
*. Correlation is significant at the 0.05 level (2-tailed).									

From the above green highlighted table values, following are inferred.

0.534 infers that there is a moderate positive opinion relationship among “To sustain as an Agile organization, relentless improvement should be part of the enterprise culture” and “To maintain agility, do you think organizational culture should encourage innovation without fear of negative consequences?”.

0.398 infers that there is a low positive opinion relationship among “To sustain as an Agile organization, relentless improvement should be part of the enterprise culture” and “To remain an Agile enterprise, it is critical to share best practices throughout the enterprise (ex: via CoP-communities of practice)”.

0.230 infers that there is a negligible opinion relationship among “To sustain as an Agile organization, relentless improvement should be part of the enterprise culture” and “It is important for business teams to operate with Agile practices to sustain enterprise agility”.

0.272 infers that there is a negligible opinion relationship among “To sustain as an Agile organization, relentless improvement should be part of the enterprise culture” and “Consistently sustaining as an Agile enterprise is a key in the digital era to compete in the market”.

0.255 infers that there is a negligible opinion relationship among “To sustain as an Agile organization, relentless improvement should be part of the enterprise culture” and “Understanding the fundamentals of the Agile mindset is crucial for all corporate personnel (across organizational boundaries) in order to sustain as an Agile enterprise”.

0.293 infers that there is a negligible opinion relationship among “To sustain as an Agile organization, relentless improvement should be part of the enterprise culture” and “The culture of creating a continuous learning supports enterprise agility”.

0.361 infers that there is a low positive opinion relationship among "To sustain as an Agile organization, relentless improvement should be part of the enterprise culture" and "In order to maintain enterprise agility, need NOT treat Agile as a strategic priority".

Similarly, among other variables, it is inferred that there is negligible and low positive opinion relationship exists.

5.3.3.4. Correlation Analysis for Hypothesis#4

Hypothesis 4: Agile methodologies are not key success factors for business & digital transformation.

Below tables shows the correlation between variables of the hypothesis#4.

Table 5. 58 Correlation for Hypothesis#4

Correlations										
		BDTransformation1	BDTransformation2	BDTransformation3	BDTransformation4	BDTransformation5	BDTransformation6	BDTransformation7	BDTransformation8
BDTransformation1	Pearson Correlation	1	.198*	.253**	.278**	.142	.184*	.191*	.256**
	Sig. (2-tailed)		.012	.001	<,001	.074	.020	.015	.001
	N	160	160	160	160	160	160	160	160
BDTransformation2	Pearson Correlation	.198*	1	.144	.154	.161*	.251**	.228**	.150
	Sig. (2-tailed)	.012		.070	.052	.042	.001	.004	.058
	N	160	160	160	160	160	160	160	160
BDTransformation3	Pearson Correlation	.253**	.144	1	.472**	.208**	.402**	.291**	.271**
	Sig. (2-tailed)	.001	.070		<,001	.008	<,001	<,001	<,001
	N	160	160	160	160	160	160	160	160
BDTransformation4	Pearson Correlation	.278**	.154	.472**	1	.398**	.200*	.290**	.240**
	Sig. (2-tailed)	<,001	.052	<,001		<,001	.011	<,001	.002
	N	160	160	160	160	160	160	160	160
BDTransformation5	Pearson Correlation	.142	.161*	.208**	.398**	1	.299**	.302**	.267**
	Sig. (2-tailed)	.074	.042	.008	<,001		<,001	<,001	<,001
	N	160	160	160	160	160	160	160	160
BDTransformation6	Pearson Correlation	.184*	.251**	.402**	.200*	.299**	1	.246**	.100
	Sig. (2-tailed)	.020	.001	<,001	.011	<,001		.002	.207
	N	160	160	160	160	160	160	160	160
BDTransformation7	Pearson Correlation	.191*	.228**	.291**	.290**	.302**	.246**	1	.339**
	Sig. (2-tailed)	.015	.004	<,001	<,001	<,001	.002		<,001
	N	160	160	160	160	160	160	160	160
BDTransformation8	Pearson Correlation	.256**	.150	.271**	.240**	.267**	.100	.339**	1
	Sig. (2-tailed)	.001	.058	<,001	.002	<,001	.207	<,001	
	N	160	160	160	160	160	160	160	160

*. Correlation is significant at the 0.05 level (2-tailed).

**. Correlation is significant at the 0.01 level (2-tailed).

From the above green highlighted table values, following are inferred.

0.198 infers that there is a negligible opinion relationship among “Agile scaling promotes digital transformation at the enterprise level” and “Agile project management techniques do NOT support successful business and digital transformation”.

0.253 infers that there is a negligible opinion relationship among “Agile scaling promotes digital transformation at the enterprise level” and “The use of Agile methodologies in marketing activities is critical for business transformation”.

0.278 infers that there is a negligible opinion relationship among “Agile scaling promotes digital transformation at the enterprise level” and “Applying Agile practices in HR functions is important for successful business and digital transformation”.

0.142 infers that there is a negligible opinion relationship among “Agile scaling promotes digital transformation at the enterprise level” and “Adapting to best Agile practices increases the happiness index of employees”.

0.184 infers that there is a negligible opinion relationship among “Agile scaling promotes digital transformation at the enterprise level” and “Agile aids in the streamlining and improvement of business processes”.

0.191 infers that there is a negligible opinion relationship among “Agile scaling promotes digital transformation at the enterprise level” and “Agile helps in the development of adaptable governance frameworks that can support business and digital transformation”.

0.256 infers that there is a negligible opinion relationship among “Agile scaling promotes digital transformation at the enterprise level” and “Factors like Customer-centricity, design thinking, built-in quality, and an innovation mindset contribute to effective digital transformation”.

Similarly, among other variables, it is inferred that there is negligible and low positive opinion relationship exists.

5.3.3.5. Correlation Analysis for Hypothesis#5

Hypothesis 5: Agile adoption is not key to achieve enterprise business agility and overcome digital transformation challenges.

Below tables shows the correlation between variables of the hypothesis#5

Table 5. 59 Correlation for Hypothesis#5

Correlations								
		Business Agility1	Business Agility2	Business Agility3	Business Agility4	Business Agility5	Business Agility6	Business Agility7
Business Agility1	Pearson Correlation	1	.654**	.276**	.257**	.356**	.282**	.201*
	Sig. (2-tailed)		<,001	<,001	.001	<,001	<,001	.011
	N	160	160	160	160	160	160	160
Business Agility2	Pearson Correlation	.654**	1	.291**	.321**	.352**	.211**	.039
	Sig. (2-tailed)	<,001		<,001	<,001	<,001	.007	.627
	N	160	160	160	160	160	160	160
Business Agility3	Pearson Correlation	.276**	.291**	1	.073	.134	.130	.188*
	Sig. (2-tailed)	<,001	<,001		.357	.090	.100	.017
	N	160	160	160	160	160	160	160
Business Agility4	Pearson Correlation	.257**	.321**	.073	1	.741**	.418**	-.071
	Sig. (2-tailed)	.001	<,001	.357		<,001	<,001	.370
	N	160	160	160	160	160	160	160
Business Agility5	Pearson Correlation	.356**	.352**	.134	.741**	1	.536**	.021
	Sig. (2-tailed)	<,001	<,001	.090	<,001		<,001	.795
	N	160	160	160	160	160	160	160
Business Agility6	Pearson Correlation	.282**	.211**	.130	.418**	.536**	1	.020
	Sig. (2-tailed)	<,001	.007	.100	<,001	<,001		.803
	N	160	160	160	160	160	160	160
Business Agility7	Pearson Correlation	.201*	.039	.188*	-.071	.021	.020	1
	Sig. (2-tailed)	.011	.627	.017	.370	.795	.803	
	N	160	160	160	160	160	160	160
**. Correlation is significant at the 0.01 level (2-tailed).								
*. Correlation is significant at the 0.05 level (2-tailed).								

From the above green highlighted table values, following are inferred.

0.654 infers that there is a moderate positive opinion relationship among "Agile allows firms to better manage change and eliminate waste, which can help to reduce development costs" and "Agile encourages greater teamwork and communication which can lead to successful results".

0.276 infers that there is a negligible opinion relationship among "Agile allows firms to better manage change and eliminate waste, which can help to reduce development costs" and "Agile does NOT assist IT businesses in delivering business value more quickly and efficiently".

0.257 infers that there is a negligible opinion relationship among "Agile allows firms to better manage change and eliminate waste, which can help to reduce development costs" and "Agile practices will help minimize the VUCA (volatile, uncertain, complex, ambiguous) challenges".

0.356 infers that there is a low positive opinion relationship among "Agile allows firms to better manage change and eliminate waste, which can help to reduce development costs" and "Agile helps to foster a more open and collaborative culture in business organizations".

0.282 infers that there is a negligible opinion relationship among "Agile allows firms to better manage change and eliminate waste, which can help to reduce development costs" and "Agile adoption aids in overcoming employee cross-cultural barriers, which promotes digital transformation".

0.201 infers that there is a negligible opinion relationship among "Agile allows firms to better manage change and eliminate waste, which can help to reduce development costs" and "Agile practices such as Management 3.0, OKRs (Objectives and Key Results) help improve business agility".

0.741 infers that there is a high positive opinion relationship among "Agile practices will help minimize the VUCA (volatile, uncertain, complex, ambiguous) challenges" and "Agile helps to foster a more open and collaborative culture in business organizations".

-0.071 infers that there is a negligible opinion relationship among "Agile practices will help minimize the VUCA (volatile, uncertain, complex, ambiguous) challenges" and "Agile practices such as Management 3.0, OKRs (Objectives and Key Results) help improve business agility".

0.536 infers that there is a moderate positive opinion relationship among “Agile helps to foster a more open and collaborative culture in business organizations” and “Agile adoption aids in overcoming employee cross-cultural barriers, which promotes digital transformation”.

Similarly, among other variables, it is inferred that there is negligible and low positive opinion relationship exists.

5.3.4 Regression Analysis

Regression is a statistical technique for building a model and analyzing the relationships between the dependent and independent variables. It examines the degree to which two or more variables are connected. To do this, hypothesis testing is applied (Wikipedia contributors, 2022b). The linear regression test is followed by the appearance of 4 major tables in SPSS ver.29 as following: Variable table, Model summary, ANOVA, Coefficients of regression.

According to Thrane (2019), there are several table components which are considered relevant to interpret the regression results, those components and rule of thumb is described below.

R-value shows how well the dependent variable and demographic factors (independent variable) go together. If R-value ranges from -1 till +1. If value is -1 then there is no correlation between dependent and independent variables. If value is 0 then there is no correlation between dependent and independent variables. If value is above 0 and <=1 then there is a correlation between dependent and independent variables.

R-square is square of the R-value. the adjusted R-square shows how different the results of the sample are from the results of the whole population. It also shows how general the results are. There must be at least a small difference between R-square and Adjusted R-square.

P-value/Sig value: Most studies use a level of significance of 5% or a 95% confidence interval. So, the p-value needs to be less than 0.05.

F-ratio: It shows how much better it is to predict variables by fitting the model after taking into account how inaccurate the model is. If the value is more than 1, it means that the F-ratio model is a good one.

"Degrees of freedom," which is sometimes shortened to "df," is the number of different pieces of data that are used to calculate a statistic. It is found by taking the sample size and subtracting the number of constraints.

If Sig. < 0.05, the null hypothesis is rejected. If Sig. > 0.05, the null hypothesis is accepted. If the null hypothesis is rejected, that means there is an effect. If a null hypothesis, on the other hand, is accepted, it means that there is no effect.

In the upcoming subsections, these values are shown for each of the hypothesis and inferences are explained.

5.3.4.1. Regression Analysis for Hypothesis#1

Null Hypothesis#1: Overcoming Agile adoption challenges is not important to implement Agile and transform as an Agile Enterprise.

Table 5. 60 Regression for Hypothesis#1

Variables Entered/Removed[a]

Model	Variables Entered	Variables Removed	Method
1	DemographicProfile_C[b]	.	Enter

a. Dependent Variable: Challenge_C
b. All requested variables entered.

Model Summary

Model	R	R Square	Adjusted R Square	Std. Error of the Estimate
1	.284[a]	.080	.075	1.985

a. Predictors: (Constant), DemographicProfile_C

ANOVA[a]

Model		Sum of Squares	df	Mean Square	F	Sig.
1	Regression	54.439	1	54.439	13.817	<,001[b]
	Residual	622.536	158	3.940		
	Total	676.975	159			

a. Dependent Variable: Challenge_C
b. Predictors: (Constant), DemographicProfile_C

Coefficients[a]

Model		Unstandardized Coefficients B	Unstandardized Coefficients Std. Error	Standardized Coefficients Beta	t	Sig.
1	(Constant)	25.860	1.428		18.105	<,001
	DemographicProfile_C	.321	.086	.284	3.717	<,001

a. Dependent Variable: Challenge_C

Interpretation of tables value are as following: R value is 0.284 which is between 0 & +1, hence there is a positive correlation between dependent and independent variables.

These is also little difference in values between R-square and Adjusted R-square, hence this model is taken for further investigation.

Sig. value is 0.001 which is less than 0.05. Hence it is inferred that null hypothesis is **rejected**. Since null hypothesis is rejected, alternate hypothesis is **accepted**.

5.3.4.2. Regression Analysis for Hypothesis#2

Null Hypothesis#2: Agile Leadership and Agile Coaching are not critical success factors in adopting Agile & transformation in IT Companies.

Table 5. 61 Regression for Hypothesis#2

Variables Entered/Removed[a]			
Model	Variables Entered	Variables Removed	Method
1	DemographicProfile_C[b]	.	Enter
a. Dependent Variable: LeaderCoach_C			
b. All requested variables entered.			

Model Summary				
Model	R	R Square	Adjusted R Square	Std. Error of the Estimate
1	.178[a]	.032	.025	2.316
a. Predictors: (Constant), DemographicProfile_C				

ANOVA[a]						
Model		Sum of Squares	df	Mean Square	F	Sig.
1	Regression	27.631	1	27.631	5.152	.025[b]
	Residual	847.313	158	5.363		
	Total	874.944	159			
a. Dependent Variable: LeaderCoach_C						
b. Predictors: (Constant), DemographicProfile_C						

Coefficients[a]						
Model		Unstandardized Coefficients		Standardized Coefficients	t	Sig.
		B	Std. Error	Beta		
1	(Constant)	31.822	1.666		19.096	<,001
	DemographicProfile_C	.228	.101	.178	2.270	.025
a. Dependent Variable: LeaderCoach_C						

Interpretation of tables values are as following: R value is 0.178 which is between 0 & +1, hence there is a positive correlation between dependent and independent variables.

These is also little difference in values between R-square and Adjusted R-square, hence this model is taken for further investigation.

Sig. value is 0.025 which is less than 0.05. Hence it is inferred that null hypothesis is **rejected**. Since null hypothesis is rejected, alternate hypothesis is **accepted**.

5.3.4.3. Regression Analysis for Hypothesis#3

Null Hypthesis#3: Sustaining as Agile enterprise is not important in digital era.

Table 5. 62 Regression for Hypothesis#3

Variables Entered/Removed[a]

Model	Variables Entered	Variables Removed	Method
1	DemographicProfile_C[b]	.	Enter

a. Dependent Variable: SustainAgile_C
b. All requested variables entered.

Model Summary

Model	R	R Square	Adjusted R Square	Std. Error of the Estimate
1	.231[a]	.053	.047	2.321

a. Predictors: (Constant), DemographicProfile_C

ANOVA[a]

Model		Sum of Squares	df	Mean Square	F	Sig.
1	Regression	47.991	1	47.991	8.909	.003[b]
	Residual	851.109	158	5.387		
	Total	899.100	159			

a. Dependent Variable: SustainAgile_C
b. Predictors: (Constant), DemographicProfile_C

Coefficients[a]

Model		Unstandardized Coefficients B	Unstandardized Coefficients Std. Error	Standardized Coefficients Beta	t	Sig.
1	(Constant)	30.120	1.670		18.035	<,001
	DemographicProfile_C	.301	.101	.231	2.985	.003

a. Dependent Variable: SustainAgile_C

Interpretation of tables values are as following: R value is 0.231 which is between 0 & +1, hence there is a positive correlation between dependent and independent variables.

These is also little difference in values between R-square and Adjusted R-square, hence this model is taken for further investigation.

Sig. value is 0.003 which is less than 0.05. Hence it is inferred that null hypothesis is **rejected**. Since null hypothesis is rejected, alternate hypothesis is **accepted**.

5.3.4.4. Regression Analysis for Hypothesis#4

Null Hypothesis#4: Agile methodologies are not key success factors for business & digital transformation.

Table 5. 63 Regression for Hypothesis#4

Variables Entered/Removed[a]

Model	Variables Entered	Variables Removed	Method
1	DemographicProfile_C[b]	.	Enter

a. Dependent Variable: BDTransformation_C
b. All requested variables entered.

Model Summary

Model	R	R Square	Adjusted R Square	Std. Error of the Estimate
1	.207[a]	.043	.037	2.233

a. Predictors: (Constant), DemographicProfile_C

ANOVA[a]

Model		Sum of Squares	df	Mean Square	F	Sig.
1	Regression	35.409	1	35.409	7.099	.009[b]
	Residual	788.085	158	4.988		
	Total	823.494	159			

a. Dependent Variable: BDTransformation_C
b. Predictors: (Constant), DemographicProfile_C

Coefficients[a]

Model		Unstandardized Coefficients B	Unstandardized Coefficients Std. Error	Standardized Coefficients Beta	t	Sig.
1	(Constant)	30.988	1.607		19.282	<,001
	DemographicProfile_C	.259	.097	.207	2.664	.009

a. Dependent Variable: BDTransformation_C

Interpretation of tables values are as following: R value is 0.207 which is between 0 & +1, hence there is a positive correlation between dependent and independent variables.

These is also little difference in values between R-square and Adjusted R-square, hence this model is taken for further investigation.

Sig. value is 0.009 which is less than 0.05. Hence it is inferred that null hypothesis is **rejected**. Since null hypothesis is rejected, alternate hypothesis is **accepted**.

5.3.4.5. Regression Analysis for Hypothesis#5

Null Hypothesis#5: Agile adoption is not key to achieve enterprise business agility and overcome digital transformation challenges.

Table 5. 64 Regression for Hypothesis#5

Variables Entered/Removed[a]

Model	Variables Entered	Variables Removed	Method
1	DemographicProfile_C[b]	.	Enter

a. Dependent Variable: BusinessAgility_C
b. All requested variables entered.

Model Summary

Model	R	R Square	Adjusted R Square	Std. Error of the Estimate
1	.187[a]	.035	.029	2.075

a. Predictors: (Constant), DemographicProfile_C

ANOVA[a]

Model		Sum of Squares	df	Mean Square	F	Sig.
1	Regression	24.666	1	24.666	5.730	.018[b]
	Residual	680.178	158	4.305		
	Total	704.844	159			

a. Dependent Variable: BusinessAgility_C
b. Predictors: (Constant), DemographicProfile_C

Coefficients[a]

Model		Unstandardized Coefficients B	Unstandardized Coefficients Std. Error	Standardized Coefficients Beta	t	Sig.
1	(Constant)	27.417	1.493		18.363	<,001
	DemographicProfile_C	.216	.090	.187	2.394	.018

a. Dependent Variable: BusinessAgility_C

Interpretation of tables values are as following: R value is 0.187 which is between 0 & +1, hence there is a positive correlation between dependent and independent variables.

These is also little difference in values between R-square and Adjusted R-square, hence this model is taken for further investigation.

Sig. value is 0.018 which is less than 0.05. Hence it is inferred that null hypothesis is **rejected**. Since null hypothesis is rejected, alternate hypothesis is **accepted**.

5.3.5 Summary of Hypothesis Results

Below table shows the summary of null and alternate hypothesis.

Table 5. 65 Hypothesis Results Summary

S. No.	Null Hypothesis Statement	Sig Value	Null Hypothesis (Rejected / Accepted)	Alternate Hypothesis (Rejected / Accepted)
1	Overcoming Agile adoption challenges is not important to implement Agile and transform as an Agile Enterprise.	0.001	Rejected	Accepted
2	Agile Leadership and Agile Coaching are not critical success factors in adopting Agile & transformation in IT Companies.	0.025	Rejected	Accepted
3	Sustaining as Agile enterprise is not important in digital era.	0.003	Rejected	Accepted
4	Agile methodologies are not key success factors for business & digital transformation.	0.009	Rejected	Accepted
5	Agile adoption is not key to achieve enterprise business agility and overcome digital transformation challenges.	0.018	Rejected	Accepted

Considering the rejection of null hypothesis, this study confirms the alternative hypotheses as below.

1) Overcoming Agile adoption challenges is very important to implement Agile and transform as an Agile Enterprise.
2) Agile Leadership and Agile Coaching are very critical success factors in adopting Agile & transformation in IT Companies.
3) Sustaining as Agile enterprise is very important in digital era.

4) Agile methodologies are key success factors for business & digital transformation.
5) Agile adoption is key to achieve enterprise business agility and overcome digital transformation challenges.

Hence, with this research I would like to confirm that Agile Leadership and Agile Coaches, Business teams, Technical, business analysis & architecture team members, Executive Level Leadership and stakeholders of enterprise need to give more emphasis on above points in order to adopt Agile and sustain as an Agile Enterprise.

CHAPTER – 6

6. FINDINGS AND RECOMMENDATIONS

6.1. Finding of the Study

Majority of the survey respondents are Male and majority fall between age groups 30-40 and 40-50 years. 100% of participants working in IT sector. 33.1%, 30%, 22.5% and 14.4% are from the following regions respectively Europe, Americas, Asia Pacific and Middle East/Africa. All survey respondents are working in IT sector. 76%, 22% & 1% respondent's years of experience is between above 5 years, 3-5 years & 2-3 years respectively. Majority (96%) of respondents are participated in Agile Transformation.

77%, 8%, 7% & 7% respondents are working in a following organization culture respectively self-organizing and self-managing, self-governance, led by manager & self-designing. 77% & 23% of are working in an organization which is practicing Agile above 5 years & between 2-3 years respectively.

Highest first majority of respondents (60%) are in Scrum Master/Agile Coach/Agile Transformation Consultant roles, second majority respondents (13.5%) are in Business Analyst/Business Manager/Product Manager/Product Owner roles. Third majority respondents (10%) are in Vice President/Management or Executive Leadership roles. Rest others are in Project/Program Manager and Team Leader/Architect roles.

As per the survey results, Scrum takes first place in the most used Agile framework, SAFe (Scaled Agile Framework) takes the second, ScrumofScrums takes the third, Kanban takes the fourth, DevOps/DevSecOps takes the fifth, Xtreme Programming

(XP) takes sixth, Scrum@Scale takes seventh and Hybrid Agile Framework takes eighth position.

According to the survey respondents, top 5 main reasons for adopting Agile are: Regular feedback cycle increases value creation, Better Quality, Productivity Increase, Faster time to market and Business/IT Alignment.

According to the survey respondents, top 5 challenges faced during Agile transformation are: Insufficient Training, Lack of collaboration, Organizational Culture, Lack of Experience and Absence of Agile Coach.

An astonishing 100% of respondents agreed that leadership is a significant aspect in determining the success of Agile transformation, which was plainly visible. Inter-team communication is seen by a resounding majority of respondents as being crucial to the success of Agile transitions. This demonstrates the urgent necessity for continued attention to open communication and teamwork between the involved teams. The vast majority of survey participants understand that investing in talent is essential for an Agile transformation to be successful and that not doing so can be a significant barrier. According to survey findings, there is broad agreement that unclear roles and responsibilities hinder successful Agile transformation. The vast majority of respondents agree that having the appropriate tools is essential for a successful Agile transition. They also agreed that overcoming employee resistance while implementing an Agile workplace can be difficult. It is clear that many people think that applying Agile concepts correctly will result in adoption and use that is successful. When pursuing an Agile transformation, organizations may find themselves in challenging terrain. In order to successfully execute these problems, which range from insufficient training to resistance to change, insufficient resources or experience, and pressure from management on desired results, a personalized strategy supported by expertise and awareness of the methodologies involved is needed.

Agile Leadership requires well-defined communication around the change vision and openness to an Agile approach in order for it to be successful. This strong consensus highlights the importance of leading from the front for successful Agile leadership. Agile leaders who opt for decentralized decision making, which entails transferring authority to where the relevant information is available, have earned overwhelming agreement from survey participants. A clear majority of survey respondents demonstrated unequivocal support for Agile leaders taking the initiative to address organizational impediments. Training, coaching and mentoring on Agile practices and Agile mindset should be provided by Agile Coaches is essential for successful Agile transformation, earned overwhelming agreement from survey participants. Participants also voted overwhelming agreement that Agile coaches should closely work with business stakeholders simultaneously working with rest of the organization, similarly Agile coaches must regularly assess the business agility and recommend the best product engineering practices.

A striking majority of respondents concurred that businesses must constantly work to improve if they want to stay flexible and competitive. Businesses that want to be Agile should encourage innovation without worrying about the consequences. Businesses must promote a culture of knowledge sharing if they want to stay flexible and competitive. Agile approaches have been cited by a sizable majority of respondents as being essential to fostering and maintaining corporate agility. All sizes of businesses are coming to understand how crucial it is to maintain agility and nimbleness in order to successfully navigate the modern digital terrain. Fundamentals Agile mindset must be understood by all corporate people if organizations need to maintain agility across all departments. Promoting a learning culture can be crucial in assisting businesses in becoming more Agile. Enterprise agility cannot be sustained without being given strategic priority, according to an astounding majority of respondents.

A startlingly large majority of survey participants acknowledge the importance of Agile scaling in advancing digital transformation at the corporate level. The vast majority of responders strongly disagreed with the idea that Agile project management approaches are ineffective for supporting successful business and digital transformation, demonstrating a professional comfort level with this popularized approach. The respondents also agreed that Agile approaches are crucial for successful corporate transformation and strongly supported their usefulness in marketing operations. The respondents think that adopting Agile practices in HR departments is essential for realizing successful business and digital transformation outcomes. According to the survey results, most participants are aware of how Agile methods can increase employee happiness. The vast majority of respondents strongly favor Agile, with the vast majority agreeing that it improves and streamlines business operations. Agile is an effective tool for assisting businesses in creating robust frameworks to support successful business and digital transformation. All of the respondents agreed that a successful digital transformation path requires a focus on the needs of the customer centricity, design thinking, and built-in quality. Additionally, it was believed that having an innovative attitude was essential to long-term success.

The overwhelming majority of respondents believe that Agile is the best method for effectively managing change and avoiding waste in order to minimize development costs, making it the obvious choice among respondents. The respondents think that the Agile methodology encourages greater levels of cooperation and communication among teams, which can result in very successful solutions. The participants vehemently disagreed that Agile does not assist IT organizations in more quickly and effectively realizing commercial value. The respondents are optimistic that Agile techniques can provide practical solutions to deal with the corporate environment's growing volatility, uncertainty, complexity, and ambiguity (VUCA). Business organizations have embraced Agile procedures to a large extent due to their benefits in establishing open and collaborative cultures. Adopting an Agile methodology is a crucial component of successfully integrating and advancing digital transformation across cultural boundaries. The vast majority of respondents think that adopting Agile principles like Management 3.0 and OKRs (Objectives and Key Results) can improve corporate agility. Agile methodologies benefit businesses in a variety of ways, including higher quality standards and increased efficiency. They can also result in quicker paths to market and enormous prospects for value generation, all the while guaranteeing successful alignment between business units and IT teams. Agile solutions also provide more efficient product delivery procedures along with improved HR & marketing operations.

6.2. Recommendations of the Study

Business and Digital Transformation in IT Sector is a dynamic and ever-changing process, which poses significant challenges to any organization. The dynamic nature of the digital transformation process brings about certain reluctance from the leadership team when it comes to embracing innovation. The dynamic environment requires strong leadership, competent personnel, effective strategies and consistent execution with respect to the goals set by the organization.

In today's fast-paced world, it is necessary for organizations to stay ahead of the competition by implementing the right strategies, tools and processes that suit their needs. This means continually adapting to changes and taking advantage of new technologies as they become available. With this in mind, leaders must be able to identify opportunities, anticipate trends and create a vision for how their business will evolve over time.

Leadership plays an important part in any successful Agile & digital transformation project as it provides clarity on goals, outlines a roadmap for progress and sets clear objectives so everyone knows what they should be working towards. Good leadership also creates an environment where team members feel supported; this leads to better collaboration between departments which optimizes processes while increasing employee engagement levels at the same time. Additionally, strong leadership encourages innovation which is critical in today's competitive landscape as organizations need differentiating factors that make them stand out from the rest.

Leaders also need to understand their customer base, think creatively about how technology can help them meet customer needs and anticipate future market trends. They must also have the capability to manage change across departments or divisions, which requires strong communication skills. Leadership is especially important when it comes to Agile & digital transformation as it helps organizations respond quickly when faced with new challenges or opportunities.

Adopting Agile methodologies can provide businesses with a framework for digital transformation by allowing teams to deliver projects faster and more efficiently than ever before. Agile brings about transparency between different departments, encourages collaboration among teams and allows for faster problem solving through continuous feedback loops. By using Agile methods such as Scrum or Kanban, businesses can reduce risk while improving quality at the same time. Additionally, leaders play an important role in driving agility within the organization by setting expectations around timescales, project requirements and resources needed to complete tasks on time.

To ensure success when undergoing digital transformation within an organization, it is essential that Agile methodologies are adopted with effective leadership guiding every step of the way. Leaders must be able to develop a strategic vision based on customer needs while setting clear objectives so everyone knows what they should be aiming for during each phase of development. Furthermore, good communication skills are essential as it ensures all departments are kept up-to-date with any changes taking place throughout the process in order to maintain efficiency throughout every stage of digital transformation.

Leadership is often responsible for setting the vision for digital transformation and guiding its implementation within the organization. Leaders must ensure that they understand how change will affect their staff and equip them with the skills needed to succeed in this new environment. They must also create an atmosphere of acceptance and trust among their employees so that they are willing to embrace and adapt to new technology solutions. Additionally, leaders need to be able to communicate their vision clearly so that everyone understands why change is necessary in order for a successful transition to take place.

At times, there can be a lack of understanding or even resistance towards adopting new technologies among some members of an organization's workforce. This reluctance can sometimes be due to fear of job loss resulting from automation or simply due to a lack of knowledge regarding how new technologies work. In such cases, leadership should focus on providing education as well as encouragement for employees who may be hesitant about embracing digital transformation initiatives.

Leaders play a critical role in ensuring that all stakeholders have access to relevant data needed for making informed decisions related to digital transformations projects. This includes not only financial data but also customer feedback, competitor analysis, market analysis, etc., all of which are essential pieces of information needed for successful business operations in today's digital world.

Furthermore, leadership should prioritize collaboration between internal teams as well as external partners so that everyone involved has an opportunity to contribute their expertise towards achieving successful outcomes. It is essential that leaders foster cooperation among all stakeholders including customers, suppliers, colleagues etc., in order for collective success throughout the entire process.

Finally, Agile adaption requires regular reassessment and review of processes within organizations as well as staying up-to-date on new technologies and trends within the industry - something which leaders must actively advocate for and encourage across teams within their company if they wish for it to stay competitive in today's dynamic business environment. Overall agility is essential if organizations are striving towards success through digital transformation initiatives – this means having dynamic leadership teams who can adjust quickly according changing industry needs while promoting collaboration between stakeholders involved in any given project or initiative.

6.3. Limitations of the Study

This study is limited to the Agile Adaption and Role of Leadership in Business and Digital Transformation in IT Sector. It is unable to address other dynamic aspects of the industry such as new technologies and innovation, which could lead to dynamic changes in the way businesses operate.

In addition, this study does not measure or assess any change in attitudes or behaviors from the respondents, who may be reluctant to embrace digital transformation or Agile adaptation. This reluctance could have a significant impact on how successful an organization's transition will be. Despite these limitations, however, we are confident that our findings provide valuable insight into how organizations can best facilitate business and digital transformation within the IT sector. We hope it inspires further research into the power of leadership when it comes to embracing change and driving success in today's dynamic market.

DISCUSSION AND IMPLICATIONS

This study sheds light on how IT businesses may enhance their business and IT transformation by implementing Agile methodologies. The specific issues that IT firms encounter when implementing Agile will be identified, along with how businesses can address these challenges. This research has also looked at the advantages that IT organizations can gain from using the Agile Methodology. To successfully implement a digital transformation, the businesses must align the changes with their strategies. Numerous businesses increasingly recognize the importance of combining the IT strategy with the business plan to create what is known as a "digital business strategy."

The concept of Agile transformation is a relatively new methodology that seeks to bring about rapid development and delivery cycles, allowing organizations to remain competitive in the ever-evolving digital landscape. To realize the full potential of Agile adaptation, however, it is essential to understand the role that leadership plays in supporting such a transition. The changing nature of technology and customer needs require an organization to constantly evolve its products, services, processes, systems, and strategies. Thus, leadership must be willing and able to drive change on multiple fronts simultaneously: by creating a culture that encourages innovation; by leveraging digital technologies; by providing resources for training and upskilling employees; by fostering collaboration among teams; and finally, by setting coherent goals based on data-driven decisions.

Leaders must also adopt the right mindset when it comes to Agile adoption. Many executives tend to view it through the lens of product development only – as an iterative process focused solely on creating better products faster. Leaders need to think expansively about their vision for how Agile practices can be integrated into their organizations' wider ecosystem – from sales & marketing to HR & operations.

The success or failure of any Agile transformation effort lies largely on leaders' ability (or lack thereof) to inspire change management initiatives and foster discoverability throughout their teams. This involves not just embracing new ways of working but also helping team members understand why these changes are necessary so they feel empowered instead of overwhelmed by them.

It is important for leaders to build trust among their teams while actively encouraging experimentation and risk taking while using feedback loops as learning opportunities rather than sources of criticism or judgement. Leaders must also remember that digital transformation requires an iterative approach — each step should be seen as part of a larger journey rather than end-goals in themselves — so they should strive to provide continual support along the way instead of just setting lofty expectations at the outset without having any scalability plans in place if things go wrong.

Finally, leaders need not forget that Agile adaption is more than a technological endeavor — it also requires organizational culture shift too. Thus, leaders need to ensure clear communication between different departments along with developing effective partnerships or collaborations with external entities when necessary, such as consultancies or tech vendors whose expertise could facilitate smoother transitions or provide insights into best practices from other industries. Doing so will help create true agility within an organization – enabling quick responses towards customer needs whilst maintaining flexibility throughout different areas such as product design & development or processes like on boarding & implementation – which would help ensure long-term competitive advantage over rivals who may remain stuck in legacy workflows.

In conclusion, the role of leadership and Agile Coach in driving digital transformation and Agile adaption initiatives is critical. Successful leaders must be able to drive change across multiple fronts simultaneously while inspiring their teams with a shared vision for success. By leveraging external resources, promoting collaboration within organizations and encouraging experimentation & risk taking, organizations can ensure that they remain competitive in the digital landscape for years to come.

CONCLUSION

In order to be successful in the 21st century, organizations must be able to rapidly adapt to changes in the market. One way to facilitate this adaptation is through the use of Agile methodology. Agile methodology is a way of organizing and managing work that allows for quick and frequent adaptations to changing requirements. It involves breaking down work into small increments that can be completed quickly, and then making frequent adjustments based on feedback from stakeholders. Many organizations have started to adopt Agile methodology in order to stay competitive in today's fast-paced world. However, implementing Agile can be a challenge, especially for larger organizations with a lot of legacy systems and procedures. There are a number of different frameworks for Agile, so it is important to select one that will work best for your organization.

Once you have selected an Agile framework, you need to create a team that is dedicated to working using Agile methods. This team should be made up of people with the necessary skills and knowledge to succeed in an Agile environment. The team should also be empowered to make decisions and take risks in order to get the job done.

Training is also critical for success with Agile methodology. All members of the team need to be familiar with the framework and how it works. There are a number of different training options available, including online courses, workshops, and conferences.

Agile methodology can help organizations adapt quickly to changing conditions, but it is not without its challenges. Organizations that are successful with Agile tend to have a dedicated team that is familiar with the framework and is willing to take risks. They also have the necessary training in place so that all members of the team are up-to-date on how Agile works.

Agile transformation is an enterprise holistic and should be sustainable change. Agile adoption and Agile transformation are not only about frameworks, tools, practices or techniques; it is more of culture and mindset. Transformations are less predictable and less controllable since they frequently follow their own course and take their own time. Be Agile as you embark on your journey of Agile transformation and lead by example. Agile Transformation is not a project with a set time frame, not a goal, but a journey.

BIBLIOGRAPHY

1. Abbas, N., Gravell, A. M., & Wills, G. B. (2008). Historical roots of Agile methods: Where did "Agile thinking" come from?. In International conference on Agile processes and extreme programming in software engineering (pp. 94-103). Springer, Berlin, Heidelberg.
2. AgilityHealth. (2022, October 12). Business Agility Health & Maturity Assessment Tools. https://agilityhealthradar.com/radars/
3. Ahmad, M. O., Markkula, J., & Oivo, M. (2013). Kanban in software development: A systematic literature review. In 2013 39th Euromicro conference on software engineering and advanced applications (pp. 9-16).
4. Akkaya, B. (Ed.). (2020). Agile Business Leadership Methods for Industry 4.0. Emerald Publishing Limited.
5. Alleman, G. B. (2005). Agile project management methods for IT projects. The story of managing projects: An interdisciplinary approach, 324-333.
6. Almeida, F., Oliveira, D., & Neves, J. (2022). The Relevance of Management 3.0 in the Development of Dynamic Capabilities in SMEs. Journal of Business Ecosystems (JBE), 3(1), 1-13.
7. Alqudah, M., & Razali, R. (2016). A review of scaling Agile methods in large software development. International Journal on Advanced Science, Engineering and Information Technology, 6(6), 828-837
8. Ambler, S. W., & Lines, M. (2020). Choose Your WoW!: A Disciplined Agile Delivery Handbook for Optimizing Your Way of Working. Project Management Institute, Incorporated.
9. Ambler, S., & Lines, M. (2012). Disciplined Agile Delivery: A Practitioner's Guide to Agile Software Delivery in the Enterprise (IBM Press) (1st ed.). IBM Press.
10. Ambler, S., & Lines, M. (2020, July). Introduction to Disciplined Agile Delivery. Project Management Institute.
11. Ashmore, S., & Runyan, K. (2014). Introduction to Agile methods. Addison-Wesley Professional.
12. Attar, M., & Abdul-Kareem, A. (2020). The Role of Agile Leadership in Organisational Agility. In Agile Business Leadership Methods for Industry 4.0. Emerald Publishing Limited.
13. Axelos. (2017, pp11-32). An Executive Guide to PRINCE2 Agile. TSO, The Stationery Office.
14. Axelos. (2018). A Guide to AgileSHIFT (First edition). TSO, The Stationery Office.

15. Banijamali, A., Ahmad, M. O., Similä, J., Oivo, M., & Liukkunen, K. (2016). Empirical investigation of scrumban in global software development. In International Conference on Model-Driven Engineering and Software Development (pp. 229-248). Springer, Cham.

16. Bergmann, T., & Karwowski, W. (2018). Agile project management and project success: A literature review. In International Conference on Applied Human Factors and Ergonomics (pp. 405-414). Springer, Cham.

17. Betta, J., & Boronina, L. (2018, December). Transparency in Project Management–from Traditional to Agile. In Third International Conference on Economic and Business Management (FEBM 2018) (pp. 446-449). Atlantis Press.

18. Boehm, B. W. (1995). A spiral model of software development and enhancement. In Readings in Human–Computer Interaction (pp. 281-292). Morgan Kaufmann.

19. Bresciani, S., Ferraris, A., Romano, M., & Santoro, G. (2021). Digital transformation management for Agile organizations: A compass to sail the digital world. Emerald Group Publishing.

20. Budoya, C., Kissaka, M., & Mtebe, J. (2019). Instructional design enabled Agile method using ADDIE model and Feature Driven Development method. International Journal of Education and Development using ICT, 15(1).

21. Burke, W. W., & Litwin, G. H. (1992). A causal model of organizational performance and change. Journal of management, 18(3), 523-545.

22. Business Agility Institute. (n.d.). https://businessagility.institute/

23. Campanelli, A. S., & Parreiras, F. S. (2015). Agile methods tailoring–A systematic literature review. Journal of Systems and Software, 110, 85-100.

24. Carroll, J. (2012). Agile Project Management in easy steps. In Easy Steps Limited (pp 14)

25. Chang, M. (2010). Agile and Crystal Clear with Library IT Innovations. In VALA2010 Conference.

26. Cohn, M. (2005). Agile estimating and planning. Pearson Education.

27. Conforto, Edivandro C., et al. "Can Agile project management be adopted by industries other than software development?." Project Management Journal 45.3 (2014): 21-34.

28. Cooke, J. L. (2012). Everything you want to know about Agile: how to get Agile results in a less-than-Agile organization. IT Governance Ltd.

29. Creswell, J. W. (1998). Qualitative Inquiry and Research Design: Choosing Among Five Traditions.Thousand Oaks Sage.

30. Cronbach, L. (1951). Coefficient alpha and the internal structure of tests. Psychometrika, 16(3), 297–334.

31. Cummings, T. G., & Worley, C. G. (2014). Organization development and change. Cengage learning.

32. Cuofano, W. I. G. (2022). AgileSHIFT And Why It Matters In Business. FourWeekMBA. https://fourweekmba.com/Agileshift/

33. Damlapinar, M. (2022). Agile Analytics For Startups: The Step-by-Step Guide for Building an Agile Startup with Data Analytics. Independently published.

34. Denning, S. 2021. How new leadership succeeds in the digital age. Forbes. 14 March. Available: https://www.forbes.com/sites/stevedenning/2021/03/14/how-new-leadership-succeeds-in-the-digital-age/

35. Ebert, C., & Duarte, C. H. C. (2018). Digital transformation. IEEE Softw., 35(4), 16-21.

36. Ebinum, M. 2019. How to: business model canvas explained. Available: https://medium.com/seed-digital/how-to-business-model-canvas-explained-ad3676b6fe4a [2022, February 14].

37. Edeki, C. (2013). Agile unified process. International Journal of Computer Science, 1(3), 13-17.

38. Elacio, A. A., Balazon, F. G., & Lacatan, L. L. (2020). Digital transformation in managing employee retention using Agile and C4. 5 algorithm. no, 15217, 15217-15225.

39. Fachrunnisa, O., Adhiatma, A., Lukman, N., & Ab Majid, M. N. (2020). Towards SMEs' digital transformation: The role of Agile leadership and strategic flexibility. Journal of Small Business Strategy, 30(3), 65-85.

40. Fader, P. (2020). Customer centricity: Focus on the right customers for strategic advantage. University of Pennsylvania Press.

41. Fernandez, D. J., & Fernandez, J. D. (2008). Agile project management—agilism versus traditional approaches. Journal of Computer Information Systems, 49(2), 10-17.a

42. Ferreira, J., Noble, J., & Biddle, R. (2007, August). Agile development iterations and UI design. In Agile 2007 (AGILE 2007) (pp. 50-58).

43. Findsrud, R. (2020). An Agile approach to service innovation: creating valuable service innovation with Agile resource integration. Journal of Creating Value, 6(2), 190-207.

44. Fisher, J. M. (2005). A time for change?. Human resource development international, 8(2), 257-263.

45. Fraser, S., Lundh, E., Davies, R., Eckstein, J., Larsen, D., & Vilkki, K. (2009, May). Perspectives on Agile coaching. In International Conference on Agile Processes and Extreme Programming in Software Engineering (pp. 271-276). Springer, Berlin, Heidelberg.

46. Fuchs, C., & Hess, T. (2018). Becoming Agile in the digital transformation: The process of a large-scale Agile transformation.

47. George, B., & Williams, L. (2004). A structured experiment of test-driven development. Information and software Technology, 46(5), 337-342.

48. Gera, G., Gera, B., & Mishra, A. (2019). Role of Agile marketing in the present era. International Journal of Technical Research & Science, 4(5), 40-44.

49. Green, P. (2012, August). Adobe Premiere Pro Scrum adoption: How an Agile approach enabled success in a hyper-competitive landscape. In 2012 Agile Conference (pp. 172-178).

50. Gregory, P., Barroca, L., Sharp, H., Deshpande, A., & Taylor, K. (2016). The challenges that challenge: Engaging with Agile practitioners' concerns. Information and Software Technology, 77, 92-104.

51. Grusendorf, S. A. (2017). Book Review: Strategy 3.0: A Guide for Entrepreneurs, Millennials, Frustrated 5-Year Planners and Anyone Else Searching for Fast, Focused, and Agile Strategy.

52. Guinan, P. J., Parise, S., & Langowitz, N. (2019). Creating an innovative digital project team: Levers to enable digital transformation. Business Horizons, 62(6), 717-727.

53. Gurusamy, K., Srinivasaraghavan, N., & Adikari, S. (2016, July). An integrated framework for design thinking and Agile methods for digital transformation. In International Conference of Design, User Experience, and Usability (pp. 34-42). Springer, Cham.

54. Gutierrez, G., Garzas, J., de Lena, M. T. G., & Moguerza, J. M. (2018). Self-managing: An empirical study of the practice in Agile teams. IEEE Software, 36(1), 23-27.

55. Hajjdiab, H., & Taleb, A. S. (2011). Adopting Agile software development: issues and challenges. International Journal of Managing Value and Supply Chains (IJMVSC), 2(3), 1-10.

56. Haleem, A., Javaid, M., Singh, R. P., Suman, R., & Khan, S. (2022). Understanding Management 4.0: Roles, Applications and Advancements. Sustainable Operations and Computers.

57. Handscomb, Jaenicke, Kaur, Vasquez-McCall, & Zaidi. (2022). How to mess up your Agile transformation in seven easy (mis)steps. McKinsey & Company. Retrieved November 10, 2022, from https://www.mckinsey.com/capabilities/people-and-organizational-performance/our-insights/how-to-mess-up-your-Agile-transformation-in-seven-easy-missteps

58. Hannola, L., Friman, J., & Niemimuukko, J. (2013). Application of Agile methods in the innovation process. International Journal of Business Innovation and Research, 7(1), 84-98.

59. Hayward, S. (2021). The Agile leader: How to create an Agile business in the digital age. Kogan Page Publishers.
60. Horlach, B., Schirmer, I., & Drews, P. (2019). Agile portfolio management: design goals and principles.
61. Ihsani, R. K., & Syuhada, M. N. (2020). Organizational Development with Six-Box Weisbord's Diagnostic Model. Jurnal Ipteks Terapan, 14(2), 89-98.
62. Jack, R. (2018). Building teal organizations with servant leadership?. In Practicing Servant Leadership (pp. 187-207). Palgrave Macmillan, Cham.
63. Javdani Gandomani, T., & Ziaei Nafchi, M. (2016). Agile transition and adoption human-related challenges and issues. Computers in Human Behavior, 62(C), 257-266.
64. Johansson, C., & Bucanac, C. (1999). The v-model. IDE, University Of Karlskrona, Ronneby.
65. Joyce, A., & Paquin, R. L. (2016). The triple layered business model canvas: A tool to design more sustainable business models. Journal of cleaner production, 135, 1474-1486.
66. Junita, A. (2021). Agile HR Strategies: Prerequisite of Business Competitiveness in a Dynamic Environment. In Proceedings of the 5th International Conference on Indonesian Social and Political Enquiries, ICISPE 2020, 9-10 October 2020, Semarang, Indonesia.
67. Kandengwa, E., & Khoza, L. T. (2021). Measuring Agile software project success beyond the triple constraint. SA Journal of Information Management, 23(1), 8.
68. Kapitsaki, G.M., Christou, M. (2015). Learning from the Current Status of Agile Adoption. In: Maciaszek, L., Filipe, J. (eds) Evaluation of Novel Approaches to Software Engineering. ENASE 2014. Communications in Computer and Information Science, vol 551. Springer, Cham.
69. Kaur, K., & Jajoo, A. (2015). Applying Agile methodologies in industry projects: Benefits and challenges. In 2015 International Conference on Computing Communication Control and Automation (pp. 832-836). IEEE.
70. Khan, M. R., Fernandez, W. D., & Jiang, J. J. (2016). Is there such a thing as Agile IT program management?
71. Kleinbaum DG, Kupper LL, Muller KE. Applied Regression Analysis and Other Multivariable Methods. 2nd ed. Boston, Mass: PWS-Kent Publishing; 1988.
72. Kotter, J, P. (2014). Accelerate Discussion Guide. Kotter International
73. Küng, L. (2017). Going digital: A roadmap for organisational transformation. Reuters Institute for the Study of Journalism.
74. Lang, G. (2017). Agile learning: Sprinting through the semester. Information Systems Education Journal, 15(3), 14. 1

75. Larman, C., Vodde, B., & Jensen, B. (2017). Large-scale scrum. Dpunkt

76. Levasseur, R. E. (2001). People skills: Change management tools—Lewin's change model. Interfaces, 31(4), 71-73.

77. Lewnes, A. (2021). Commentary: The future of marketing is Agile. Journal of Marketing, 85(1), 64-67.

78. Light, M. (2009). How the Waterfall Methodology Adapted and Whistled Past the Graveyard. Gartner Research.

79. Link, P., & Lewrick, M. (2014). Agile methods in a new area of innovation management. In Science-to-Business Marketing Conference (pp. 3-4).

80. Livermore, J. A. (2008). Factors that Significantly Impact the Implementation of an Agile Software Development Methodology. J. Softw., 3(4), 31-36.

81. Lopez Martín de Blas, M. n.d. CTO Module 2 Part 1 [Lecture notes]. IE Business School.

82. Ma'arif, M. Y., Hafifi Yusof, M. F., & Mohd Satar, N. S. (2018). The Challenges of Implementing Agile Scrum in Information System's Project. Jour of Adv Research in Dynamical & Control Systems, 10.

83. Mahanti, A. (2006). Challenges in enterprise adoption of Agile methods-A survey. Journal of Computing and Information technology, 14(3), 197-206.

84. Manen, H. V., & Vliet, H. V. (2014). Organization-wide Agile expansion requires an organization-wide Agile mindset. In International Conference on Product-Focused Software Process Improvement (pp. 48-62). Springer, Cham.

85. Marchand, D. A., & Wade, M. (2014). Digital business transformation: Where is your company on the journey. Perspectives for Managers, (187), 1.

86. Maretzke, M. (2019, March 11). When to use waterfall, when Agile? Agile-minds.com. https://www.Agile-minds.com/when-to-use-waterfall-when-Agile/

87. Masgo, E. (2021). What is Agile Leadership and Why is it important? Management30.com

88. Mathiassen, L., & Pries-Heje, J. (2006). Business agility and diffusion of information technology. European Journal of Information Systems, 15(2), 116-119.

89. McDonald, K. J. (2015). Beyond requirements: analysis with an Agile mindset. Addison-Wesley Professional.

90. McMackin, J., & Heffernan, M. (2021). Agile for HR: Fine in practice, but will it work in theory?. Human Resource Management Review, 31(4), 100791.

91. Mdluli, S., & Makhupe, O. (2017). Defining leadership competencies needed for the fourth industrial revolution: leadership competencies 4.0. Africa Expansion Project.

92. Memon, B. (2020). A Systematic Literature Review On Agile Coaching And The Role Of The Agile Coach.

93. Mersino, A. (2018, November 30). The Role of an Agile Leader During an Agile Transformation. Vitality Chicago Inc. https://vitalitychicago.com/blog/what-leaders-role-agile-transformation/

94. Middleton, P. (2001). Lean software development: two case studies. Software Quality Journal, 9(4), 241-252.

95. Miranda, E., & Bourque, P. (2010). Agile monitoring using the line of balance. Journal of Systems and Software, 83(7), 1205-1215.

96. Misra, S. C., Kumar, V., & Kumar, U. (2006). Success Factors of Agile Software Development. Software engineering research and practice, 1, 233-239

97. MJV Technology and Innovation. 2019. Open and closed innovation: what are the differences? [Blog, 14 June]. Available: https://www.mjvinnovation.com/blog/open-and-closed-innovation-what-are-the-differences/

98. Mohammad, S. M. (2017). DevOps automation and Agile methodology. International Journal of Creative Research Thoughts (IJCRT), ISSN, 2320-2882.

99. Moreira, M. E. (2013). Being Agile: your roadmap to successful adoption of Agile. Apress.

100. Mulder, P. (2013). Greiner Growth Model. Retrieved from Toolshero: https://www.toolshero.com/strategy/greiner-growth-model/

101. Müller, A. L., & Pfleger, R. (2014). Business transformation towards sustainability. Business Research, 7(2), 313-350.

102. Narayan, S. (2015). Agile IT organization design: For digital transformation and continuous delivery. Addison-Wesley Professional.

103. Nascimento, G. S. D., & Oliveira, A. A. D. (2012). An Agile knowledge discovery in databases software process. In International Conference on Data and Knowledge Engineering (pp. 56-64). Springer, Berlin, Heidelberg.

104. Niemi-Grundström, M. (2014). Developing, evaluating and managing library with Agile methods. Library Management, 35(6/7), 481-485.

105. Olteanu, C. G. (2018). IT Agile transformation. Academy of Economic Studies. Economy Informatics, 18(1), 23-31.

106. Omanovic, S., & Buza, E. (2013, October). Importance of stable velocity in Agile maintenance. In 2013 XXIV International Conference on

Information, Communication and Automation Technologies (ICAT) (pp. 1-8).

107. Osmundsen, K., Iden, J., & Bygstad, B. (2018). Digital Transformation: Drivers, Success Factors, and Implications. In MCIS (p. 37).

108. OxfordLearnersDictionaries.com. (n.d.)., Oxford Advanced Learner's Dictionary
at https://www.oxfordlearnersdictionaries.com/us/definition/english/Agile

109. Özkan, D., & Mishra, A. (2019). Agile Project Management Tools: A Brief Comprative View. Cybernetics and Information Technologies, 19(4), 17-25.

110. Ozkan, N., Tarhan, A., & Kucuk, C. (2017). Scrum at Scale in a COBIT Compliant Environment: The Case of Turkiye Finans IT. XP2017.

111. Parsons, D., Ryu, H., Lal, R. (2007). The Impact of Methods and Techniques on Outcomes from Agile Software Development Projects. IFIP International Federation for Information Processing, Vol 235. Springer, Boston, MA.

112. Paula. (2022) "Top 6 Challenges in Agile Transformation and Ways to Overcome Them." 6 Key Challenges in Agile Transformation and Their Solutions, 2022, premierAgile.com/Agile-transformation-challenges-and-solutions.

113. Pereira, J. C., & de FSM Russo, R. (2018). Design thinking integrated in Agile software development: A systematic literature review. Procedia computer science, 138, 775-782.

114. Perkin, N., & Abraham, P. (2021). Building the Agile business through digital transformation. Kogan Page Publishers.

115. Perminova, O., Gustafsson, M., & Wikström, K. (2008). Defining uncertainty in projects–a new perspective. International journal of project management, 26(1), 73-79.

116. Petersen, K., Wohlin, C., & Baca, D. (2009). The waterfall model in large-scale development. In International Conference on Product-Focused Software Process Improvement (pp. 386-400). Springer, Berlin, Heidelberg.

117. Poth, A., Kottke, M., & Riel, A. (2020). Evaluation of Agile team work quality. In International Conference on Agile Software Development (pp. 101-110). Springer, Cham.

118. PRINCE2 Agile in 1000 Words. (2021). Axelos.Com. https://www.axelos.com/resource-hub/white-paper/prince2-Agile-in-one-thousand-words

119. Prince2. (n.d.). PRINCE2 Methodiek | NL. https://www.prince2.com/nl/prince2-methodology

120. Principles behind the Agile Manifesto. (n.d.). https://Agilemanifesto.org/principles.html

121. Qurashi, S. A., & Qureshi, M. (2014). Scrum of scrums solution for large size teams using scrum methodology. arXiv preprint arXiv:1408.6142.

122. Rasnacis, A., & Berzisa, S. (2017). Method for adaptation and implementation of Agile project management methodology. Procedia Computer Science, 104, 43-50.

123. Razzouk, R., & Shute, V. (2012). What is design thinking and why is it important?. Review of educational research, 82(3), 330-348.

124. Rigby, D. K., Berez, S., Caimi, G., & Noble, A. (2015). Agile innovation. San Francisco: Bain & Company.

125. Ross, J.W. (2020). How to succeed without being the smartest person in the room. Available: https://cisr.mit.edu/publication/how-succeed-without-being-smartest-person-room

126. Ruiz, A. The most common mistakes in the process of management, transformation and change of the Organization.

127. Sánchez, M. A. (2017). A framework to assess organizational readiness for the digital transformation. Dimensión Empresarial, 15(2), 27-40.

128. Santos, V., Goldman, A., & Roriz Filho, H. (2013). The influence of practices adopted by Agile coaching and training to foster interaction and knowledge sharing in organizational practices. In 2013 46th Hawaii International Conference on System Sciences (pp. 4852-4861).

129. Sarangee, Kumar, et al. "Agile transformation in dynamic, high-technology markets: Drivers, inhibitors, and execution." Industrial Marketing Management 102 (2022): 24-34.

130. Scaled Agile, Inc. (2022, July 1). Benefits of SAFe: How it Benefits Organizations. Scaled Agile. https://scaledAgile.com/what-is-safe/scaled-Agile-benefits/

131. Schlömer, I. F. (2022). Agility as a Driver of Digital Transformation-a Literature Review. In Conference on e-Business, e-Services and e-Society (pp. 238-253). Springer, Cham.

132. Schober, Patrick MD, PhD, MMedStat; Boer, Christa PhD, MSc; Schwarte, Lothar A. MD, PhD, MBA. Correlation Coefficients: Appropriate Use and Interpretation. Anesthesia & Analgesia: May 2018 - Volume 126 - Issue 5 - p 1763-1768. doi: 10.1213/ANE.0000000000002864

133. Schwaber, K. (1997). Scrum development process. In Business object design and implementation (pp. 117-134). Springer, London.

134. Shore, J., & Warden, S. (2021). The art of Agile development. " O'Reilly Media, Inc.".

135. Shrivastava, S. V. (2010). Distributed Agile software development: A review. arXiv preprint arXiv:1006.1955.

136. Šmite, D., Gonzalez-Huerta, J., & Moe, N. B. (2020). "When in Rome, Do as the Romans Do": Cultural Barriers to Being Agile in Distributed Teams.

In International Conference on Agile Software Development (pp. 145-161). Springer, Cham.

137. Sohaib, O., Solanki, H., Dhaliwa, N., Hussain, W., & Asif, M. (2019). Integrating design thinking into extreme programming. Journal of Ambient Intelligence and Humanized Computing, 10(6), 2485-2492.

138. Solomon, D. J. (2000). Conducting web-based surveys. Practical Assessment, Research, and Evaluation, 7(1), 19.

139. Spayd, M., & Madore, M. (2020). Agile Transformation: Using the Integral Agile Transformation Framework to Think and Lead Differently (Addison-Wesley Signature Series (Cohn)) (1st ed.). Addison-Wesley Professional.

140. Spencer, M. H., & Winn, B. A. (2005). Evaluating the Success of Strategic Change against Kotter's Eight Steps. Planning for higher education, 33(2), 15-22.

141. Stapleton, J. (1999). DSDM: Dynamic systems development method. In Proceedings Technology of Object-Oriented Languages and Systems. TOOLS 29 (Cat. No. PR00275) (pp. 406-406).

142. State of Agile. (2021). https://stateofAgile.com/

143. Stray, V., Memon, B., Paruch, L. (2020). A Systematic Literature Review on Agile Coaching and the Role of the Agile Coach. In: Morisio, M., Torchiano, M., Jedlitschka, A. (eds) Product-Focused Software Process Improvement. PROFES 2020. Lecture Notes in Computer Science(), vol 12562. Springer

144. Stray, V., Tkalich, A., & Moe, N. B. (2020). The Agile coach role: coaching for Agile performance impact. arXiv preprint arXiv:2010.15738.

145. Streiner DL. Maintaining Standards: Differences between the Standard Deviation and Standard Error, and When to Use Each. The Canadian Journal of Psychiatry. 1996;41(8):498-502. doi:10.1177/070674379604100805

146. Strode, D. E., Huff, S. L., & Tretiakov, A. (2009). The impact of organizational culture on Agile method use. In 2009 42nd Hawaii International Conference on System Sciences (pp. 1-9).

147. Talik, Z. 2021. What is a VUCA world and how does it affect digital business? [Blog, 4 November]. Available: https://www.boldare.com/blog/what-is-vuca-world-definition [2022, January 25].

148. The Canvas Revolution. (2021, November 14). Agile Project Canvas. https://thecanvasrevolution.com/product/Agile-project-canvas

149. The Role of an Agile Leader During an Agile Transformation. (2018, December 1). Vitality Chicago Inc. https://vitalitychicago.com/blog/what-leaders-role-Agile-transformation/

150. Thompson, K. (2019). Solutions for Agile governance in the enterprise (SAGE): Agile project, program, and portfolio management for development of hardware and software products.

151. Thrane, C. (2019). Applied Regression Analysis: Doing, Interpreting and Reporting (1st ed.). Routledge.

152. Tomas, N., Li, J., & Huang, H. (2019, June). An empirical study on culture, automation, measurement, and sharing of devsecops. In 2019 International Conference on Cyber Security and Protection of Digital Services (Cyber Security) (pp. 1-8).

153. Turetken, O., Stojanov, I., & Trienekens, J. J. (2017). Assessing the adoption level of scaled Agile development: a maturity model for Scaled Agile Framework. Journal of Software: Evolution and process, 29(6), e1796.

154. Turk, D., France, R., & Rumpe, B. (2014). Limitations of Agile software processes. arXiv preprint arXiv:1409.6600.

155. Uikey, N., & Suman, U. (2012). An empirical study to design an effective Agile project management framework. In Proceedings of the CUBE International Information Technology Conference (pp. 385-390).

156. University of Barotseland, Statistics - Introduction to Basic Concepts, in bobhall.tamu.edu/FiniteMath/Introduction.html. 2014.

157. Venkatesh, D., & Rakhra, M. (2020). Agile adoption issues in large scale organizations: A review. Materials Today: Proceedings.

158. Wikipedia contributors. (2022b, November 28). Regression analysis. Wikipedia. https://en.wikipedia.org/wiki/Regression_analysis

159. Yadav, R. S. (2012). Improvement in the V-Model. International Journal of Scientific & Engineering Research, 3(2), 1-6.

160. Zaydi, M., & Nassereddine, B. (2020). DevSecOps practices for an Agile and secure IT service management. Journal of Management Information and Decision Sciences, 23(2), 1-16.

www.ingramcontent.com/pod-product-compliance
Lightning Source LLC
Chambersburg PA
CBHW060001170726
48282CB00042B/682
9789391209001